PRINCIPLES OF E-EDUCATION VOL III

Social Dimensions of
E-Communication

Social Dimensions of E-Communication

Michael H. Foox

iUniverse, Inc.
New York Lincoln Shanghai

Social Dimensions of E-Communication

iUniverse books may be ordered through booksellers or by contacting:

iUniverse
2021 Pine Lake Road, Suite 100
Lincoln, NE 68512
www.iuniverse.com
1-800-Authors (1-800-288-4677)

I IIS Publishing Company is a trademark of IIS LLC
246 North Main Street
Spring Valley New York
NY 10977

ISBN-13: 978-0-595-35656-0 (pbk)
ISBN-13: 978-0-595-80134-3 (ebk)
ISBN-10: 0-595-35656-7 (pbk)
ISBN-10: 0-595-80134-X (ebk)

Printed in the United States of America

CONTENTS

CHAPTER I

FROM INTERACTION TO INTERACTIVITY

1

§ 1 Introduction

Subjects and Objects

Human individuals live in worlds with objects. This seems to be so natural and evident, that the differences between subjects and objects, and implicitly also between subjects and subjects, are fundamental to every individual's psychological makeup and that of the human mind in general. A world full of *objects* appears to enforce communication between *subjects*. Subjects understand themselves as an individual—a form of understanding that is not only necessary but also totally evident.

This evidence is important in sciences, which in addition to research and experiment has communication as their main substance. Social philosophy and sociology as well as psychology, psychiatry and education are particularly involved. Is human communication indeed limited to human subjects? Focus on communication is empirically important, and a wide range of possibilities to communicate are studied, even those who entail the question whether therapeutic interventions can be realized. The same focus represents an important philosophical dimension, since the features of human communication are unique in the world of living creatures and therefore fundamental to human essence and the emergence of identity. Human relationships differ from relations between humans and non-human objects. Communications with animals, which we consider as 'friends' and have as 'pets', already demonstrate that difference, often reaching beyond articulation in words, thoughts, and expressions.

That makes it even more understandable how *relations with objects* have played a secondary role in the field of studying human communication. They are given the role of mediator, of instruments to experience the social world, to measure (or even build the basis for) human life. But they are never evaluated on equal footing with humans as far as the shape and quality of communication are concerned.

That has for a long time also been dominant in education. Although education has to create respect for the world of objects, for animals, and for nature in general, that world has never been appreciated as partners in the education process. Pets are instrumental in children's learning processes and their development of sentiments and the mind. Yet, parents cannot understand how their kids could be educated by entities other than human beings labeled 'teachers'. Pets are never teachers, they say. Education is primarily a field of communication. Communication is *exercised* in education but also *trained, unfolded, enhanced,* and *shaped into socially valuable and normatively correct skills,* which are governed by human subjects. Objects—in contrast to human subjects—play at best a secondary role in this regard.

That situation changed thoroughly nowadays—a change that marks the end of the twentieth and the beginning of the twenty-first century. Never before has the fine line between communication of human subjects and of objects influencing and shaping human communication been so thin and vulnerable. Today, especially with the exploration of virtual worlds intertwining with the worlds of so-called real facts, we no longer maintain fixed determinations of either world or reality character.

The appearance of electronic mail (an electronic technique with unforeseeable consequences and global dimensions, which emphasizes the importance of the fast growing Internet as a concretion of Cyberspace) is an eloquent example of developments in the near future. Communication seems no longer restricted to, and the privilege of, two (or more) human subjects. But if objects with a new identity, such as computers nowadays seem to have, are recognized as factors that create communication, then this change is also relevant to education. It should influence all levels of communication and all institutional settings that deal with the subtleties involved. Computers are often nothing but an instrument and categorized at the same level as a calculator, a radio, a walkie-talkie or an overhead projector. One day they will shape human communication perhaps more deeply, decidedly, and swiftly than a teacher ever is able to do.

Interaction, Interactivity—A First Glance

It is a fascinating thesis that computers, together with other electronic devices, will change our concept of *interaction* (between two fixed human identities) into *interactivity* (between a human identity, an e-device, and a changed human identity that creates new features of identity under the influence of the e-devices). *Interactivity is in that case a new emancipating power of the human mind, which results from educating human subjects as citizens of a society in which electronics became a major influence.*

There is consequently no way to deny that new qualities of communication create new social structures. Those new structures display correlating new character features of new citizens. However, one also cannot deny that the process of education itself transcends such important changes in human consciousness and social practices. Teachers may have to change their attitudes, and accept the world of electronics as a constitutive element of their education. The qualities and implications of human communication in a world shaped by objects (such as computers and related e-devices) do enter the domain of human communication. But this does not imply the dissolution of education as a predominating social activity. And it certainly does not announce a socially organized disappearance of the teacher's function. *The transition from interaction into interactivity includes a new pedagogic differentiation, based on new forms and insights in communication.* Teachers with special skills in maintaining electronic devices and in mastering the computer-related language complete the range of modern educational knowledge and proficiencies.

However, it must be clear that a cultural resistance to objects, in particular electronic mechanistic devices (are computers mechanisms of a new kind?) as elements of human communication, plays a role today. *Mechanization* is a term of abuse in many contexts.

In the early days of industrialization, for instance in the English 17th century textile industries, workers destroyed the spinning machines made of cast iron. Those machines were symbols of a mechanization that threatened their jobs and income, and the new enemies of the future of their children and their working class culture. Our modern computers are not made of cast iron, and are not destroyed by our office workers, but uncertainty and cultural criticism are also widespread.

There is a fascinating dichotomy in the appreciation of our developing world of electronic devices. On the one hand, a deep and multidimensional fascination has the younger generation in its grip, whereas disorientation pertaining to ethical standards and to basic human qualities is fervently alive. But on the other hand, the concept belongs to e-mechanization and the coming cultural revolution, which will lead to new types of communication, education and work. The outcry "interaction, yes, interactivity, no!" is not unimaginable.

Let us not forget, that the fascination for the *automaton* dates back to the days of the Ancient Greek culture. The same fascination was revived in the European Renaissance, where Queens and Kings possessed parks and gardens with automatic clockworks, automatic water decorations, and mathematically designed labyrinths, which pleased and astonished the royal guests. Each court of a king or an emperor had gifted mathematicians and philosophers to design mechanic calculators, which enabled them to solve complex mathematical and astrological problems and to find out about wars and fates. Later on, concepts like 'automation' or 'cybernation' were widely used, misused, and debated during the early 1960s. Uses and debates of these concepts threatened the industrialized world immediately after WW II, when many countries (especially in Western Europe) were changing from an agrarian to an industrial economy and life style.

It is important to emphasize that our awareness of a transition from 'interaction' to 'interactivity' emerges at the end of the twentieth century, and at great distance from any positive or negative appreciation of the automation process in an a fully industrialized society. "Interactivity" is *neither* the product of automation, *nor* the indication of an upcoming technological culture, but specifically a characteristic of new dimensions in human communication. In other words: *interactivity belongs to our understanding of changing properties of human communication* and is not a fad belonging to the encompassing technological culture at the end of the millennium.

That is the basis to admit and accept the issue in the context of education, which is the privileged place where communication skills are trained to inhabit human minds and behavioral patterns. Do not forget that the personal life stories of individuals at the turn of this century are woven with many different threads: cultural, ideological, social, psychological, and economic ingredients are the basis for formatting our youth. And one of these threads, the cultural, is in itself a multi-layered construction.

Sherry Turkle has convincingly brought to light that progressing social and moral layers in society (such as the envisaged transition from interaction to interactivity) contain slower developing layers in context, so that different logics always influence all types of progress. That is undoubtedly the case in a technologically enhanced education discourse, which goes hand in hand with the emergence of interactivity.

This colors the fact that many mixed ideas, opinions, public relations puffery, policies, and cyber designs accompany the development of interactivity in the field of social communication theories and their background philosophy[i], as for instance in symbolic interactionism[ii]. One of the predominant opinions that color the landscape of often contradicting metaphors is in the understanding of computers as belonging to interaction between man and machine (if computers are machines at all!).

Sir Leon Bagrit[iii] formulated the general opinion of the sixties and the early seventies in Western society in his 1964 BBC Reith Lectures. "It is not a question of machines replacing man: it is largely a question of extending man's faculties by machines so that, in fact, they become better men, more competent men," he stated. Today one considers whether computers are really machines like "The Spinning Jenny" in the English industrial revolution in the 17th and 18th century, or whether they are solely instruments to enhance human qualities.

Papert's opinion, formulated approximately two decades later, is radically different when he describes his virtual "Knowledge Machine" and states that a computer may unleash children's learning capacities[iv]. However, the general tendency is yet to proclaim the agonizing choice between extending man's capacities or to alienate and dehumanize. One cannot deny the fact that, even today, there is this agony in the background of the unfolding thesis that *interactivity is a new form of human communication, which cannot evolve without e-devices, computers in the first place.* Does this agony destroy the thesis about interactivity and it's belonging to the world of e-devices?

Are Computers Machines?

Keep in mind: computers are not cast iron machines! But they long have been treated like machines, and many people have thought they were! Only at the end of the century have computers engendered the question of whether they are machines at all, even whether they are material objects.

Our fascination is definitely a cultural issue: *are they like us,* perhaps not in form, but in function? They may be even more perfect than any human being can be—but is that enough to say that they are "only and purely objects"? Indeed, a computer is not a perfect lover, a great thinker, or an inspiring musician. What then is there to say about intelligence and communication? If they *are* not better, they just *do* better, and show at the least a "domain betterment", one could say. They do a lot more than we do when they become partners in communication, and often perform at the speed of light! Is what they do really communication or do they nothing more than providing us improvement of our communication? Is that the case, and will it always be the case, even in the near electronic future? Let us not write a list of questions without end.

Even if we regard computers and related e-devices as purely material objects, they are more than that and perform decidedly better and differently than we do! So the word "partner" seems appropriate: computers and e-devices are different from us but enough like ourselves to accomplish communicative situations. This challenges us to leave the concept of interaction behind and come to terms with interactivity.

It is clear—all this is not about simple objects or about a reality that exists completely beyond our selves, our souls and our minds. It is a story of change. It might also be a story of our changing self! The change pertains to the outside world, but is also vitally relevant for our worlds inside our selves. We, as subjects, change because of the changing world of objects. And there are apparently parts of that world that are neither subject nor object, but go-betweens that influence us enormously, in particular with regard to our communicative abilities. That is important in recognizing the concept of interactivity. And all this seems to happen in a broader context, because the change from interaction to interactivity takes place in a changing social world!

So one must observe that there is no interactivity without e-devices, which we have firmly acknowledged as a partner in our human communications. If one restricts communication solely to human subjects, then one enters the realm of *dialectics* as a theme of thought formation and of the dynamics of thought processes, which makes it a truly philosophical theme. But it seems impossible to encounter those concrete dialectics without recurring to the practices of communication, which show an importantly wider scope. They include subject to non-subject relations. The practices of communications between subjects in the field of education are extensively researched and described. But the relations in which the non-human subjects, the computers, participate, are not studied sufficiently. How does the machine, transformed into a constitutive force in human communications, work?

§ 2 Automation

Automation by means of electronics was perceived in the middle of the sixties as an achievement to extend the abilities of man, embracing first the technical and later also the spiritual dimensions of human existence.

That idea was born in the period of cultural criticism about the new technology, and developed in accordance with a range of anxieties pertaining to the question of whether the essence of man was not threatened by this evolution. Are machines taking over some of the most delicate human qualities? Faustian scenes were depicted, and a veil of pessimism was spread over those who dared to openly proclaim that electronic devices carry new opportunities with them for social enrichment, above all in education and communication.

The 1964 BBC Reith Lectures

Automation

One of the most famous among those optimistic authors was the renowned British industrial and technology specialist Sir Leon Bagrit, who was invited in 1964 to deliver the Reith BBC Lectures on computers and their general application. He sensed the spiritual climate of those days, a spirit that really belongs to the history of our becoming acquainted with computers. His opening sentence was therefore: "For many people, automation is a terrifying word."

As computer and automation were identical in those days, it is not surprising that he speaks (and goes on speaking throughout) about computers in terms of a machine. "It conjures up visions of tyrannical machines reducing man to the status of a mere pusher of buttons or watcher of dials, and abolishing the need for human thought and judgment. I can sympathize with those fears, but I am sure that they are unjustified. We are not destined to become a race of babysitters for computers. Automation is not a devil, a Frankenstein. It is no more than a tool, but a tool of such immense possibilities that no one can yet see the full extent of what it might achieve for mankind."

Needless to say how we live today beyond looking at computers as a tool, and agree with the idea that computers, symbolizing the entire domain of electronics, direct and guide us into mankind's future. On the basis of this early observation, one should already have perceived that there is no youth without immersion in the world of computers and no education without acceptance of computers as a partner for students and teachers alike. However, the emphasis on human features in contrast to any 'machine' was too important, so that time had not come for this conclusion.

The human mind was not yet ripe for accepting forms of a non-organic life as a partner-in-human-life, and the computers were too big, too expensive, and also too far from the public to be thus accepted. Listeners to the BBC in 1964 were exceptionally a regular user in close contact with computers. Hence Bagrit's observation: "There is a great technological explosion around us, generated by science" is rather a wake-up call then a pessimistic description of the culture of that time. The following remark: "We shall need to apply our scientific and technological resources to literally every aspect of our society, to our commerce, our industry, our medicine, our agriculture, our transportation" became a cornerstone of life at the end of the century, and led to a continuous 'extension of man'.

A sharp insight worth mentioning is in the second paragraph of Bargit's first lecture. It says: "Automation in its true sense is brought to fruitful fruition only through a thorough exploitation of its three major elements: communication, computation and control—the three 'C's." And the author begins at home when he exemplifies the need to maintain the 'C's' in the example of a steel industry—not explicitly aware of the historic dimensions of his example, which reach back to the UK industrial revolution. Automation as an activity that relies upon communication and control as well as foresight in required developments (delivered by computers) leads to a more profound assimilation of technological applications in the fabric of social life.

Man-Machine Partnership

It all does, however, engage new dimensions of man-machine partnerships. Bargit observed them in the control of processes and operations, hitherto relying solely upon man as a control agent. But he is a prudent observer, and anxious not to destroy man's self-image pertaining to his eventual mastership. He adds: "In each case, careful preparation and operational research are essential to achieve a fruitful man-machine relationship, so that the machine is given only those parts of the task which it can do best and the integrity and importance of final human judgment and decision is preserved."

It is most important to be aware of how those sentences maintain an entire vision on human quality and eventually the essence of man. The machine is given a task; man decides. The machine does what he can do best; man decides what is the best in a given case. The man-machine relationship is fruitful insofar as a sound division of tasks to perform is designed. And for all this, an appropriate combination of hardware and software (already words in Bagrit's vocabulary) seems necessary! A lack of knowledge and understanding of computers as mechanisms with specific qualities leads to no results or at the very most to catastrophic effects. Human intelligence gives the lead, there is no awareness whatsoever that this leading position could change and machines become understood or managed like human brains.

Although the man-machine relationship is mentioned throughout his lectures, there is no idea that this relationship is in essence a very specific and precious type of communication in its own right. This communication is unique in human history. It results in a hitherto unknown partnership between human brains on the one hand and machine—or computer brains on the other. The two brains are not identical, but the use of the expression is only partially metaphorical. The unsolved riddle that is also ours is in the metaphor, which is only partially metaphor and partially material reality. The same riddle is in the use of the concept of 'communication'.

Education

"We must make tremendous efforts to ensure that our economic and political thinking is contemporary with our opportunities and that we are not crippling ourselves with an out-of-date pattern of education", Bagrit concludes in his third lecture. It means that education, as a specific form of communication, receives his full attention[v].

The question remains, however, what one understands by education and what role is given to automation by means of computers and related e-devices (although the Reith lectures only focus on computers). One reads: "The real problems of education are going to center on the need to develop people capable of living the fullest possible lives in an age of plenty". This does underline the *products* of education: 'people capable of…' but not the *changing structure* of education itself. Again: "We shall have to produce men and women who are able to understand the significance of the past, who are in the stream of current ideas and who can make use of them, and who have the quality of imagination that is capable of foreseeing and welcoming the future." The basics of such an education process, in particular relating to qualitative changes in our understanding of communication, are not focused.

The BBC listeners were able to listen to many proposals to enhance education, but none touched the issue of communication itself. It would, however, have been feasible to imply that issue, for instance where 'day boarding schools' were proposed. Those schools would create a new education environment, a full day from breakfast to evening, and "during this much lengthened school-day…it should be easier to instill in them the type of attitudes which are necessary if we are going to develop the social conscience and sense of social responsibility which an age of plenty is going to demand".

There is thus a heavy emphasis on *integration* of knowledge from various disciplines, the arts and social practices included. But will such an effort ever be successful with individuals who neglect the enormous impact of social relations and their communicative essence?

Even these proposals pertaining to a change in the time budget of the students and the changing attitude in schools are, how relatively small and simple, forever bouncing back a predominant thought pattern. "We are so accustomed to thinking in terms of poverty and of the allocation of resources within an atmosphere of scarcity, that to suggest this kind of education on a wide scale will…" encounter the idea that we cannot pay for it. Scarcity is the issue at stake. To think in terms of scarcity is an epistemological imperative in Western society at large.

The question is whether communication is a topic that fits this thought pattern. That is indirectly at stake where Bagrit puts forth the dynamics of automation with its widespread computer use. That dynamic makes a shift possible from poverty-in-scarcity towards wealth-in-scarcity, because he expects automation technology to become the greatest wealth-creating power on earth.

That was proclaimed in 1964. Today nobody dares to embrace that thesis. Electronic technology has been sinking so deep into all layers of our consciousness, and became so intertwined with human life and its mode of existence, that we cannot single out what is produced by e-technology and what by non-e—technology. The change brought forth by e-technology has been so radical that these distinctions no longer work.

It remains therefore important to underline how the BBC lectures formulate as major concerns (1) a genuine breadth of education, and (2) an enhanced sense of human responsibility. The two are closely linked to the qualities of communication in modern society. Bagrit is very close to this conclusion, when he consequently underlines that "politics are not only the concern of politicians. They necessarily involve the general mass of citizens, and I believe that it is an urgent political task to educate the people as a whole to make them aware of the broad problems and the opportunities of automation. With the support of public opinion, we must strive for a national policy on this issue."

However, it does not contain a challenge to tackle the quality of communication as a result of the introduction of electronic devices in human interrelations. It's even not sufficient when, as Bargit concludes, "we can make sure that there is enough automation to give society the free time and the wealth through which we expose people to the opportunity of self-development."

The problem is apparently not feasible in terms of quantities, neither of free time nor of less workload, but in the correlated changes in the image of man. Is a human being today, with the speedy developments of e-technology, able to change his self-appreciation by means of accepting this computer-related technology as a partner in human communication patterns? A transition from interaction to a continuous state of interactivity would be the ultimate sign of such acceptance.

§ 3 Skinner's Teaching Machines

Education is what survives when
what has been learnt has been forgotten
B.F.Skinner

Skinner (1904–1990), the well-known US psychologist and behaviorist, designed boxes in which animals were automatically rewarded for behavior, such as depressing a lever or pushing a button. Unlike Pavlov, he did not change a behavior through stimuli but through rewarding acts that approached the desired behavior.

Operant Conditioning

He concluded that such 'operant conditioning' could be used to shape behavior in more general terms. That leads immediately to changes in communicative behavior, and learning or educating is an icon of those changes. Skinner started with pigeons that roosted outside his office window at the University of Minnesota, where he took an academic position in 1936 and wrote his book *The Behavior of Organisms*. The pigeons moved in accordance with his stimulus-response system, and he observed how his behaviorist viewpoint made sense. His favorite was teaching pigeons to bow! Behavior he positively reinforced reoccurred, and intermittent reinforcement appeared to be particularly effective.

So pigeons, so daughters! Skinner did the same with his own daughter, the older of two, for which he developed a "baby box", also named the "air crib", which was in fact no more than a controlled environment chamber for infants. "The box was a combination of a crib and a playpen with glass sides and air conditioning, but looked too much like keeping a baby in an aquarium to catch on", he wrote later, but the effects of positive and negative reinforcement on behavior were there[vi]! Dividing a task into small parts, learning intellectually as well as emotionally each part at a time, and then stretching the parts erratically was very successful. The same method counts for sensitization and desensitization of specific behavior and anxieties, phobias, and panic reactions, for instance the anxiety in flying an airplane.

The procedure of sensitization and desensitization is even today a basic element of behavioral therapy in psychology and psychiatry. Skinner developed teaching machines whereby students could learn bit by bit, and give an answer whereby each bit was immediately rewarded. He would have been greatly satisfied to see how today computers deliver programs for self-instruction on the basis of his principles. It would be worthwhile to consider how much of our computer-related environment relies upon truly behaviorist principles.

Teaching Boxes

So one needs not be astonished to find teaching machines in Skinner's behaviorist activities. In fact, details of computer-dependent communications are committed to all types of behaviorist philosophy, which focuses exclusively the appearance of communicative acts and leaves out internal processes that produce the appearance. Behavior is caused by external factors, behaviorism proclaims, and everything we do in a communicative context relates to our experiences of reward and punishment. The mind, as opposed to the brain, does not exist beyond communication, behaviorism claims. Even linguistic phenomena are susceptible to a strict system of rewards and punishments. If that is the real frame for learning, educating and communicating, what then do electronic machines contribute? Can these ever do anything other than reinforce the behaviorist impetus?

Skinner first provides an answer about education in general. There are three basic metaphors in his theory: (1) growth/development, (2) acquisition, and (3) construction. Today we would perhaps use other expressions, but their meaning is clear. The first is evident: humans have learned everything they know or do. Even a genetic predisposition does not replace learning. Capabilities are never enough; learning has to awaken them. Acquisition provides the growth/development. Everyone has to receive an education, whatever form and content it takes.

Skinner notices[vii]: "These conceptual maneuvers are necessary because neither growth nor acquisition correctly represents the interchange between organism and environment. Growth is confined to one variable—the form or structure of behavior—and acquisition adds a second—the stimulating environment; but two variables are still not enough, as the inadequacies of both stimulus-response and information theories show. Superficially, the exchange between organism and environment may be viewed as a matter of input and output, but difficulties arise…neither metaphor tells the teacher what to do or lets him see what he has done. No one literally *cultivates* the behavior of a child as one cultivates a garden or *transmits* information as one carries a letter from one place to another."

This leads to another idea, which is often contested. Skinner introduced his third expression, *construction*, and defends that position as follows. A teacher informs the student in the sense that his behavior is given form or is shaped. But the student constructs that behavior in relation to his environment. Essential for the structure of communication is the fact "that teaching can be understood as an arrangement of contingencies of reinforcement. Left alone in a given environment, a student will learn but he will not necessarily have been taught. The school of experience is not a school at all, not because no one learns in it, but because no one teaches. Teaching is the expediting of learning;

a person who is taught learns more quickly than one who is not. Teaching is most important, of course, when the behavior would not otherwise arise."

It is clear that these factors represent essential parts of any set of contingencies of reinforcement, constituting the essence of education as well as of communication. Learning by doing emphasizes the *response*; learning by experience the *occasion upon which the response occurs* and learning by trial-and-error, the *consequences*.

Skinner envisaged on this basis the construction of his "boxes" in view of education and communication in general. They promise an effective control of behavior, not in the form of a disinterested study of changes in behavior and environment, but rather an active manipulation of those changes.

Learning Machines

"Education is perhaps the most important branch of scientific technology. It deeply affects the lives of all of us. We can no longer allow the exigencies of a practical situation to suppress the tremendous improvements which are within reach", Skinner said, and developed his theory that complex behaviors and communication segments should be reduced to smaller units: "The whole process of becoming competent an any field must be divided into a very large number of very small steps, and reinforcement must be contingent upon the accomplishment of each step. This solution to the problem of creating a complex repertoire of behavior also solves the problem of maintaining the behavior in strength."

A year later, McLuhan[viii] attempted a more encompassing view on the cultural significance of electricity and electronic machinery. He claimed as an elaboration of Skinner's remarks: "Automation is not an extension of the mechanical principles of fragmentation and separation of operations. It is rather the invasion of the mechanical world by the instantaneous character of electricity. That is why those involved in automation insist that it is a way of thinking, as much as it is a way of doing."

Reading those lines, one sees how our modern computers operate exactly in this manner without showing us their fragmentation processes and without consulting us about the efficiency in transferring our communications into binary codes. It happens without our knowledge or consent, whereas Skinner still struggles with the issue because of the low level of technical perfection of boxes and machines. But he acknowledges how "it has been found that the contingencies of reinforcement, which are most efficient in controlling the organism cannot be arranged through the personal mediation of the experimenter. An organism is affected by subtle details of contingencies, which are beyond the capacity of the human organism to arrange. *Mechanical and electrical devices must be used*" (our italics)[ix].

Skinner seems to have had our computers in mind when he reflects upon the imperfections of the early learning machines. Today's computers do not show us anymore the inherently behaviorist approach to human communication. None of us has a *total* knowledge about the processes on which these electronic machines rely. An example is, that early learning machines to teach arithmetic are described without paying attention to the fact that such a learning process relates to communication processes. In fact, it is described as if there is no communication at all, and that is most surprising.

In other words, the early machines appear as a solipsistic adventure. Take a text with the first figure of his 1969 book *The Technology of Teaching*, which appears in the square window on a paper tape. Reduction of reality is the catchword here. The student causes figures to appear in these holes by moving sliders, and when the right sliders have been moved, the equation is complete. The machine senses the answer, and if it is correct, a new frame appears. A counter may be added to tally wrong answers.

Other teaching machines are more complex, combining spelling and arithmetic on the same principle and with the same techniques, but they remain solipsistic machines. The reinforcement of the right answer in these machines is immediate, progress depends on the student's own rate, not on the patience or impatience of the teacher, and progress to a complex repertoire is created automatically.

So, after all, "there seems no reason why a classroom should be any less mechanized than, for example a kitchen. A country which annually produces millions of refrigerators, dishwashers, automatic washing machines, automatic clothes dryers, and automatic garbage disposals can certainly afford the equipment necessary to educate its citizens to high standards of competence in the most effective way", Skinner adds eloquently.

The truth of his statement is still an issue of political decision and of the politics of education in general. Is automation politically acceptable and legally correct? Skinner even reinforces his statement as if he foresees our contemporary worries and debates: "We cannot prepare young people for one kind of life in institutions organized on quite different principles. The discipline of the birch rod may facilitate learning, but we must remember that it also breeds followers of dictators and revolutionists."

Is Nature a Binary World?

A Skinner reference to Rousseau gives us some important afterthoughts about the uses of our computers in modern communication networks, especially in education. "Use only those forms of coercion or punishment which arise naturally from the student's behavior; if he breaks a window, do not repair it. But let him experience a cold room. Use only natural rewards. Social reinforces cannot be neglected, alas, but they can at least be genuine."

There are indeed many questions about the quality and essence of human communication. Computers and related e-devices do hide from our eyes how much they rely upon the binary system of awards and punishments. Do we ever realize the impact of the binary world when we operate the keys of our computer keyboards? Their binary character seems at distance to the poetic words and sensitive expressions we put into those machines to communicate or to safeguard them. How would our sentences read if we were continuously aware about the inherent binary reductions? And, more fascinating, can our computers, used as communication machines, ever be 'natural' to us? Do they become a way of thinking and doing, so that they became our 'second nature'? They could do that despite their imminent binary character, neurologists tell us. This forms a major challenge to our understanding of human communication, which undoubtedly started with the research and ideas of Skinner!

§ 4 The Children's Machine

Do our computers in any way have to do with our human nature, and is that relationship in any way important for a restatement pertaining to the essence of human communication? The question was Skinner's and will be encountered again several times. Papert's often quoted book that bears the title of this paragraph suggests from the very beginning, that children have a different and closer relationship with computers, electronic games, and related e-devices than their parents normally have[x].

The Entryway to Computers

"Video games are toys—electronic toys, but not doubt, toys—and of course children like toys better than homework. By definition, play is entertaining and homework is not. What some parents may not realize, however, is that video games, being the first example of computer technology applied to toy making, have nonetheless been the entryway for children into the world of computers...Video games teach children what computers are beginning to teach adults—that some forms of learning are fast-paced, immensely compelling, and rewarding. The fact that they are enormously demanding of one's time and require new ways of thinking remains a small price to pay (and is perhaps even an advantage) to be vaulted into the future. Not surprisingly, by comparison school strikes many young people as slow, boring, and frankly out of touch[xi]."

Educative Communication in Context

Education, being a particular form of communication, has always entailed a moment of change. More than a century ago, the psychologist William James proclaimed: "You make a great, a very great mistake, if you think that psychology, being the science of the mind's laws, is something from which you can deduce definite programs and schemes and methods of instruction for immediate schoolroom use. Psychology is a science, and teaching is an art; and sciences never generate arts directly out of themselves. An intermediary inventive mind must make the application, by using its originality".[xii]

We need an intermediary inventive mind? This sentence is true, but one has to bear in mind that, since James, (1) psychological experimentation has grown and produced valuable insights and conclusions, whereas (2) the latest electronic communication technology appears to do the same. Can computers and their sophisticated programs become the "intermediary mind" James referred to? And is this only feasible under the condition that we radically change our philosophical ideas and practical insights pertaining to human communication? Any affirmative viewpoint still has to show the many paths to go to sustain the expansion of our ideas on communication. Is the transition from interaction to interactivity one of those ideas?

Such a transition is certainly in need of practical and spiritual preparation. One cannot change the basic structures of communication in one day, or all will be lost in the flow of social events. Papert quotes John Dewey, the icon of American education, who, more than hundred years ago, envisaged a more active and self-directed style of learning and living for the American school. The climate for change in schools was in his days as unfavorable as today, although the motives might have been slightly different. The vision of a child as a person with the right to intellectual self-determination may have been strong in theory, but the social practice was disappointingly different.

Social and educational conservatism were the major power against change in Dewey's times, whereas nowadays dissatisfaction with the system and its techniques of self preservation go hand-in-hand with a resistance to new forms of communication, in particular to electronic communication. The question remains: "in trying to teach children what adults want them to know, does school utilize the way human beings most naturally learn in non-school settings?" Papert brought an important issue to the fore, saying: "The computer is offering new opportunities to craft alternatives. Will public education lead the way or, as in most things, will the change first enhance the lives of the children of the wealthy and powerful and only slowly and with much effort find its way into the lives of the children of the rest of us? And will school adapt to an epistemological pluralism?"[xiii]

Growing Computer Literacy

This question of a great divide between computer-literates and computer-illiterates today seems less urgent. Computers are less costly and many learning institutions have systems to financially provide the devices to the students. And, what is more, life with a computer has become more intensive than ever, particularly in the younger generation. They put computer games, the acquiring of information through special programs, watching films and photos, reading texts and chatting with others, on a single line called 'daily life'.

That such a life embraces an electronically enabled lifestyle and depends on highly on the computer does not seem to play a major role. There is hardly a decisive distinction anymore between the 'haves' and the 'have-nots' since there are game halls, phone shops, and Internet cafés in a nearby future in each town and all over the globe. Papert foresaw this situation and created the idea of a virtual Knowledge Machine, inspired by Negroponte's experiments and designs of such mechanisms.

Computers as a Life-style

He envisaged in essence a machine that nowadays exists everywhere: an electronic device that puts all knowledge available in the hands of everyone who has the literacy to access and decipher. "Knowledge" means "data" in this context, and does not presuppose an identical global understanding and interpretation of those data. If that were a fact, differences in culture and native language would evaporate with the introduction of the machine.

The opposite has happened. Global knowledge and mastering of facts goes strongly with a new appreciation of local knowledge and lifestyles, just as the formation of large state unions (for example, the European Union) not only leads to the dissipation of the national state, but at the same time accentuates a renewed interest in the region. As a consequence, the regions in Europe produce economic wealth, and are often regions, which form cross-boarder units. Let us not forget that such lifestyles are forms of communication, so that these observations touch our subject directly.

This is mirrored in the fact that Papert can consider, how "the educational development of children is therefore seen as rigidly dependent on learning to read in a timely way. The prospect of the Knowledge Machine suggests that this basic assumption may not be necessarily true for all time, and indeed may start to unravel within a decade or two. I am not suggesting that the written language is likely to be abandoned. I am suggesting that new thinking is needed about the position assigned to it as the prerequisite to the accumulation by students of useful knowledge, or at least as the first route to be opened to children when they begin their formal education."

In the light of actual developments one has to say that the Knowledge Machine should be a computer, which functions in the context of an e-educative environment. The contemporary Human Genome Project uses computers as elements of sequencing machines that locate and visualize genes. In the same manner, one should say, will computers become elements of an electronic education environment, transforming the relation between "Machine and Child" into "Machines with 'Children with Machines'"

In Other Words

The 'Knowledge Machine', if that artifact could ever focus the essentials of human communication, should change its name. The distinction between 'Machine and Child' or 'Machine and Student' on one hand, and "Machines with 'Children with Machines'" on the other suggests how the future of education is in the construction of *environments* rather than in the use of individual *machines*. Machines, not unlike Teachers, are single elements, which become inadequate for education as soon as one observes the qualitative changes in communication.

These qualitative changes, their demand in education as well as their realization within the accelerated growth of electronic devices, might solve the tensions between the *constructivist* and the *instructionist* subculture in pedagogy. How? It becomes inadequate to ask whether the student is the active subject and the teacher the passive, or conversely the student the passive consumer and the teacher the producer. This question has long been discussed in the field of education, and answered in opposite directions. But the epistemological pattern never changed. The basic pattern that supports the understanding of communication shows this resistance to change. It is a pattern constructed in essence by two elements, which form the polarity between teacher and student, machine and child, Subject and subject. One conclusion seems very important indeed. Take the already mentioned example: as long as we engage single computers to decipher the Human Genome, we will never complete it's reading.

As long as we engage single computers to create a pattern of human communication, we will never change education. The key is in a change of communication towards forms that transcend the dichotomies involved. Such an attitude found its expression in the creation of an electronic environment, in which sequences of computers perform differently, create new structures, and come up with new results. Those sequences, together with a further integration of related e-devices, also create a new educational environment in which neither a teacher nor a student is active or passive. That new patterning of communication leads to new ways to study and teach mathematics, language, and other classical school subjects. And it leads away from machine feedback, as if with them the question-and-answer approach becomes endlessly duplicated under the name 'communication'.

§ 5 Citizens

The mentioned changes in form and substance of communication are also changes in the experience of *citizenship* in a modern world. Without automation no change is feasible from *interaction* (together with the classical feedback mechanisms and other dualistic interpretations of human as well as mechanic (inter-relationships) towards *interactivity*.

The concept 'interactivity' itself was seldom used before the 1990s, and the recent publication of T. Morrison's compendium *The Magic of Interactive Entertainment* was really an eye-opener[xiv]. However, the basics for this concept were laid down in the technological developments of the so-called 'interactive media'. Do not forget how our powerful media machinery *presents* things or issues in such a manner that one is inclined to forget how they are *created* instantaneously.

The time lag is abolished and a new directness takes its place. And *presentation* blurs the traditional *ontological* question of whether 'what is there' is 'really and objectively there'. This happens so 'naturally' that one is not attempted to think about its backgrounds or implicit theoretical substance.

Citizens

One of the most important individuals involved in communication is the citizen. Citizens must by definition communicate in State and Society. It is difficult, nowadays, to determine what citizens precisely are; "you and me" would be the most simple and understandable answer, but that expression has many different layers of meaning. And many different discourses come together in the concept of a citizen.

There is the discourse of everyday life, in which subjects communicate and from time to time need to emphasize forms of communality. These are normally provided by a national State or by other State-like structures, such as a Region or a Province. All public places and public functions are for citizens, and here we meet the legal discourse in function, as well as the political, to order and arrange the public space. Citizens are therefore subjects of law and as legal subjects also of politics. In view of their responsibility and liability in law, they possess individual rights and have obligations to fulfill. The ways in which they have rights and fulfill obligations may differ, but the necessity to fulfill remains a common issue all over the Western world and many other parts of the globe.

With this need come ethical, political, psychological, and other dimensions in which exists a great diversity of communication patterns. The managing of critical phases in economy and social life, an outstanding issue in today's Western culture, requires a complexity of various discourses, with moral as well as technical, legal and economic problems. To overcome critical situations is often considered a task for politicians who must rely upon the cooperative attitude of citizens—at least, that is the general scenario of modern society.

Important here is that this scenario only works with a high degree of consensus among citizens. That consensus is not only based upon a well-coordinated whole of intentions and will, but in the first place upon an overarching political theory. Philosophers always tried to provide such a political theory. One could describe the outlines of Western philosophy from Plato to Popper in terms of this need for a theory—which has, apart from its genuine philosophical profile, also a political importance that leads to questions pertaining to the quality of human communication.

That quality is nowadays seen in context with virtues, values, freedom, and political as well as social responsibility. It is astonishing how, after the encompassing Marxist theoretical designs, political philosophy started to spin around liberal ideas with almost universal pretensions. And it surprises how for that reason the foundations of a political philosophy focus the problems of communication. Questions pertaining to communication are, however, exclusively raised in view of their effectiveness and implicated binding force, rather than in view of their substance and foundation. Do we really need such considerations, and focus solely the internal structure of communication in times where we need to emphasize much more the need for an almost universal effect of communication? That is a critical question, which seems correct and logical if one considers the conflicting world we live in.

Ask politicians—they complain how nobody is interested in the means of communication that are provided, and only the effects of communicating seem to count. This is the more important since politics refer to *images* of reality, which are in the main created and maintained by legal decisions and the epistemology, which confirms the existing legal order. Political reality is suggested to be the reality we have to live in, and that image is predominantly legal. Interests in society, who energize communication, are only effective when their presentation is legally correct. Political discourse is therefore closely linked with legal discourses. And it is legal theory as well as legal scholarship that deliver the essential points of interest in communications.

'Self' and 'Others'

The distinction between 'self' and 'others', so vital for any attempt to understand human communication, is therefore normally defined in harmony with legal epistemology. The distinction is based upon a relation between two independent entities and leads, from the days of Thomas Hobbes (1588–1679) on, to a specific social geometry that elucidates the communicative potency of human individuals as a force to bind two independent and autonomous entities named 'individual'. Philosophers in later centuries such as Immanuel Kant and G.W.F.Hegel confirmed this idea and used it as the blueprint to explain social life in general. John Rawls has, in his famous *Theory of Justice (1971)*, re-used this approach for a predominant *contractual* interpretation of human communication and togetherness. Rights of individuals are the building blocks of society.

A further element of the distinction between 'self' and 'others' is in the important revaluation of the Enlightenment idea as forwarded in Kant's famous essay *"What is Enlightenment?"* (1784). That text inspired Habermas as well as Foucault to reflect upon the presuppositions of social life and its communicative structures. Habermas claimed that Kant's essay shows how the Enlightenment is still an inspiring force in modern social thinking. It is a major feature of modernity to accomplish the Enlightenment, he suggests. This consideration leads to the *category subject* as the basis for modern thinking and modern life, a category that is outreaching to other subjects and thus creates communicative structures with its 'self' as point of departure and point of return.

However, Kant's posthumous papers consider a human person not solely in legal and individualistic terms. What does this mean? Can one accomplish the project of Enlightenment without changing the understanding of a human subject? One can probably not. That's evidently a matter of self-reflection, which not only focuses the *self* as an autonomous force, but also the *other* as an element that is not a simple doubling of the self.

Every human person is an individual that needs *recognition,* which comes by definition from other persons. This recognition constitutes a human person and is not exclusively based on a possession of rights, but is prior to rights. Kant's essay puts the coming-into-being of a person in the hands of others. That is a physiological, a psychological and a social process, which he determines as *recognition* ("Achtung"). The latter surpasses morality, law, rules and laws, so that a human person is not subjected to law from its very beginning of life in society.

Consider Paul Ricoeur's adage in his 1990 publication *Soi-même comme un Autre*, translated as: *Oneself as Another*. His words of the book's title explain a viewpoint that is inherent to Kant's position: "The self does not know itself immediately, but only indirectly by the detour of the cultural signs of all sorts which are articulated on the symbolic mediations which always already articulates actions, an, among them the narratives of every-day's life".

The structure of a 'self' cannot be understood without the presence of others. My self-consciousness emerges in the recognition of others. In that esteem, which is the basic element of recognition, I discover my identity as a person that is able to recognize another person, which includes a discovery of the multiplicity of my 'self'. Communication has the same structure: *to communicate is an act that implies a change of my 'self'.*

It seems unnecessary to underline the importance of this viewpoint. Human communication carries the problems of centuries-long interpretations of the essence of human life, the 'self' and the 'other' included. Political life, being the backbone of social life in general, maintains an image of man that tells how individual rights form the nucleus of human life in social contexts. Is it not a shame that contemporary philosophers have to spend so much energy in showing the inadequacy of this image? Their remarks are not only relevant for law and society, psychology and economy, but also for human communication.

Charles Taylor wrote in this context: "The kind of freedom valued by the protagonists of the primacy of rights is a freedom by which men are capable of conceiving alternatives and arriving at a definition of what they really want, as well as discerning what commands their adherence or their allegiance. What is truly important is that one be able to exercise autonomy in the basic issues of life, in one's most important commitments. Now, it is very dubious whether the developed capacity for this kind of autonomy can arise simply within the family. (...) Surely it is something which only develops within an entire civilization To know what it is to be an autonomous agent, to have one's own way of feeling, of acting, of expression is an identity, a way of understanding themselves, which men are not born with. They have to acquire it. Thus we live in a world in which there is such a thing as public debate about moral and political questions and other basic issues. We constantly forget how remarkable that is, how it did not have to be so, and may one day no longer be so".[xv] One could speak of a philosophical turn in understanding the basics of communication, if one considers these observations about citizens in a society.

New Citizens: A Turn in Understanding Communication

The turn pertains to the birthplace of a 'self', which seems not to include a natural individuality and egocentricity, but a communicative act from the very beginning of life on. Babies do not cry for egocentric purposes, but in order to express their need to be recognized. Relations are not exclusively understandable in terms of two interacting *egos* but rather in terms of one ego becoming a 'self' because of the existence of an '*other ego*'. That turn in our view of communication manifests itself in four remarkable aspects of new citizenship. We indicate these aspects only briefly, because an analysis of each of them would require a far-reaching publication of a nature that leads away from communication as the central issue.

I. First, there is an emerging new type of citizenship that relates to new features of *institutions*. They are clearly visible in recent new ideas and practices of *bureaucracy* and *administration*. The two were in earlier periods of Western civilization the only, ultimate and general, state governed way to represent each individual living in a State. The limits of the State, legally as well as geographically unassailable and a symbol of sovereignty, are today less important than ever. They are less important because of the emerging unions of National States. The European Union shows this as well as transnational Treaties and formations of economic cooperation do. A recent example is the Latin American MERCOSUR in relation with Southern Europe. They are also on the edge of losing their absolute power because of global trading, transnational production of goods and assessment of products, and—not lastly—because electronic communication simply neither knows nor recognizes State borders.

Citizens are now facing, together with traditional institutions, 'geographically non-identifiable institutions' which is especially for senior citizens often an alarming experience. Those institutions incorporate new techniques, many of them based on electronic machines, and have a different access, many of them also via electronically designed programs.

Traditional clients of such institutions are really afraid to just become electronically served, where they normally experience a moment of valuable social contacts. Take the evolution of electronic banking as an example, in particular where these electronic machines function within the architecture of a bank. Machines serve clients where in earlier days people did. Machines do not *represent* the bank, are not a *symbol* for the act of saving, do not *appreciate* the deposits of clients. Are citizens denied social contact because of the electronic techniques? And is that not a clear contrast to what was described as a turn in the evaluation of communication? Others appreciate this development because they are conducting all their banking whenever they like, much more completely and on their own initiative, and with respect of their privacy.

II Second, new features of citizenship relate to *genetics*, often combined with new insights of neuro-scientific nature and sustained by hitherto unknown electronic techniques of visualization. There is more than one issue of change involved. We highlight the following developments:

Genetics emerge into a new way of *thinking about social relations*. Problems of determinism arise, and the individual appears to carry the weight of factors that do not belong to any individuality, although the expression "genetic constellation" suggests this. Language is in any case no longer able to express all elements of genetic nature, whereas the production of genetic knowledge seems to be impossible without computer techniques. People walk around with a fundamental uncertainty about their identity in case of illness and disease. Does genetics offer a therapy, or a police-like identity search and control?

Genetics change the fundamental concept of *freedom*. How can one feel free with an unknown and unexplored package of information that at least partially relates to illness, heritage, family responsibility, and death? There is a strange mix of feelings in this regard: genetics provides freedom *from* blind chance and determinism, and freedom *to* select our actions. Do citizens ever possess enough knowledge to practice these freedoms?

Genetics shed a new light on each individual's *genealogical tree*. This fact challenges a new interpretation of the old adage "honor thy father and thy mother". This honoring is no longer honoring a family member, but pertains to oneself, who appears in the light of genetics to be an *identity with the others* in the genealogical tree! It is I who stand on the shoulders of my family, sometimes with one foot, sometimes with both feet! Honor your parents because they are in you, they are you—that would be the adequate expressiveness.

Genetics change *patterns of social relationships*. This is most manifest in the genetic consult and counseling. There is in this new medical situation no acute illness at stake, as there is neither a determinable patient nor the fulfillment of the traditional Hippocratic oath. The counseling pertains to *statistical* data and *probabilities* created by electronically performed analyses. Decisions of life and death, for instance whether an abortion should follow, depend on an *interpretation* of statistics. It is clear that one must conclude that genetic counseling changes the traditional patterns of institutionalized medicine. Problems in the future will also deal with the field of health care and health insurance.

It is not unsubstantial to emphasize that citizens will develop a new awareness about their identity and responsibility. These two important issues in the realm of communication are initiated by the omnipresence in modern society of a medicine that includes genetics. The conclusion is, that genetics causes a new civil consciousness.

III A third new type of citizenship envisages an increased awareness of the natural *environment*. Citizens are stimulated to engage in new dimensions of responsibility for the environment. This pertains not only to their reading about the melting polar caps of the globe or the coming of cyclones. Rather, the new attitude challenges a re-interpretation of the meaning of accessed natural goods such as water, air, gasoline and coal, and responsibility for their waste products. New citizens create an elaborate understanding about the fact that their relation to the environment is not a subject-object relationship. The environment is, in other words, not a *thing* to dispose of freely. Citizens are only citizens because they can *inhabit* the environment, they are together with that environment, and should take care as if it concerns a partner.[xvi]

IV A *fourth* new type of citizenship relates to *learning*. Stimuli to propagate "active citizenship" reach far beyond appeals to vote or accept public functions, and aim at participation in a "learning society". The latter involves (1) a type of *learning* that differs fundamentally from *teaching* or *instructing*, a type that is (2) *circular*, so that electronic devices and social institutions learn from the learning processes they instigate, and furthermore is (3) *long lasting*, often defined as "life-long". Social positions change accordingly (workplace homework, e-technological divide), and age barriers tend to be abolished in the learning situation (the elder have to learn as well as the young). We neglected "adult learning" as a specific social form and conceived it only as a form of learning "at a later age". *Learning society* is the concept that replaces the concept of a *contractual society* because the latter represents the concept of exchange of fixed positions!

All reflections upon new forms of citizenship have in common the turn from individualism towards a more dialogical understanding of communication. The turn itself is an important contribution to making electronic communication possible, and a fruitful conceptualization in view of foreseeable technological developments.

§ 6 Interactivity

E-education concentrates on dimensions of the e-programs and devices, which are *not* confined to information and/or amusement only. Goals beyond such items are generally described with vague terms like 'personal growth' or 'personal change'. In the case of using e-materials that are not exclusively aimed at information, change seems to gain importance. Change could be tested like the reception of information, and presented by means of analyzing the student's feedback as registered in the computer programs. Students change attitudes and other personality features through their involvement and active participation in the e-programs. As a consequence, the difference between *interaction* and *interactivity* becomes extremely important in the field of communication.

Interaction is an appropriate expression to describe all sorts of reciprocal actions. Reciprocal actors are enriched by means of reception and assimilation of data information. However, the crux of the distinction is the fact that they receive and assimilate *as fixed entities* and not *as entities in a process of continuous change*. Here is the essential difference in reciprocity within the range of entities. If e-programs only create interaction (mostly pragmatic and consumptive), then the relations remain beyond the deeper layers of an actor's life sphere, his or her emotional life, and potential for personal growth. In other words, the interaction and the learning on the basis of reception and assimilation of data do not make the actor become *a different personality*. The learning and growth of the person involved is predominantly linear.

Interactivity is not a simple circularity in contrast to the predominant linear character of interaction. The concept points at changes of life sphere, expansion of personal experiences, and growth in character and opinion, because the interaction in itself has changed. The latter is no longer between *fixed entities* but between *continuously changing entities*. The actors in interactive and multimedia e-education programs are continuously involved in the triangle "virtual reality", "life reality", and "companion other". This makes them "*inter*active" selves that develop in each phase of the process into *someone else* because the "input" changes them, so that they are a different entity when creating an "output" that is again "input" to others. The "else" in the expression "someone else" indicates the variety of positions in identity-formation when learning and interaction occur.

One cannot describe whether that entire process is (a) circular, (b) develops along other lines of representation, or (c) provokes different ordering processes. However, the outcome of the total engagement in interactivity is clearly different from what is ever feasible at each individual moment. Here again is an important point of difference with interaction. It may need the reality of case-analyses to clarify and to justify all envisaged implications.

The Interactivity-Principle

Electronic education is a specific form of interactivity, a concept that changes traditional and general views on education as it takes seriously the 'E' of 'E'lectronic, 'E'nhancement, and 'E'ducation in contrast to learning.

One could say that e-education is predominantly characterized by this principle. Interactivity embraces change and information that challenges change. It determines the lifelines of a participant in e-education and forms the building blocks for an unfinished and unachieved life-mosaic. One could, of course, speak of 'education in cyberspace'. But even if one would prefer to do so, it should be made clear how the one-sided (i.e.: non-interactive) relationships dominate most aspects of cyberspace behavior. The linear paradigm in interaction and information dominates 'education in cyberspace' as soon as it does not accept interactivity as a guiding principle.

Interactivity involves student and e-program on the basis of equality. Emphasis is on reciprocity between student and program in such a manner that the student is, *after* information, data, or other stimuli of the program or the e-activity, not the same he or she was *before*. To articulate this insight somewhat philosophically, one can say that each actual *understanding* takes place on the basis of *having understood* through a process of education and participation in a culture. That is essential for each fragment of interactivity.

Consequences of this view relate, among others issues, to testing. To test a student *changes* that student: if one tests in the traditional manner, one only can test where the student *once was*, and never *where he is* at this moment in preparation for being elsewhere in the next phase of his or her interactive behavior. The use of the concept 'interactivity' seriously involves character in this process, sustained by the many opportunities to display interactive behavior through e-educational devices.

Another consequence is that interactivity challenges the overemphasis on *instruction* (as a form of input) and *being instructed* (as a form of positioning on the basis of an output) in traditional education. Tests are, again, maintained as a privileged control mechanism, in contrast to a non-linear feedback, which would be called 'change'. This puts traditional testing in perspective and challenges us to differentiate between instructing and educating. In philosophical words, interactivity is a concept based on a positive appreciation of 'becoming' rather than 'being', on 'changing' rather than on 'positioning'.

One could distinguish at least *two* types of the notion of "interaction" and two types of the notion of "interactivity". There is a *strict*, and a *fuzzy* notion of *interaction*, and also a *strict* and a *fuzzy* notion of *interactivity*. The jargon of education in general, and of e-education specifically, does not separate these notions correctly. "Interaction" is the general expression for mutual relations. One could analyze more appropriately, and refine the distinction between the definitions of both concepts. We focus on the two extremes, which are the strict notion of Interaction and Interactivity. If $\underline{U}$ stands for User, $\underline{P}$ for computer Program, <u>Co</u> for Communication, <u>in</u> for instrumental linear relations, and <u>vice versa</u> for circular relations, then

<u>Interaction</u> *strict use* can be symbolized as

(1) Co = [U <u>in</u> P]1, [U <u>in</u> P]2…[U <u>in</u> P]n.

and

<u>Interactivity</u> *(strict use)* symbolized as

(2) Co = ((({[U <u>vice versa</u> P]1 [U <u>vice versa</u> P]2}1,> <u>vice versa</u>< {[U <u>vice versa</u> P]1 [U <u>vice versa</u> P]2}2)),…((({[U <u>vice versa</u> P]1 [U <u>vice versa</u> P]2},> <u>vice versa</u>< {[U <u>vice versa</u> P]1 [U <u>vice versa</u> P]2}))n.

The gradual transition from "<u>in</u>" to "<u>vice versa</u>", from the informative to the formative, plays a dominant role in these formulas. (1) is entirely dominated by this "<u>in</u>"-formula, whereas (2) is radically determined by the "<u>vice versa</u>". The "<u>vice versa</u>" in (2) opposes the formulations of (1). The difference between the two is fundamental. One could venture to systematically analyze how U and P change under the influence of each other's existence. That is easier to perceive in the case of (1), which is used in ordinary language in a great variety of meanings, than in (2) where one would expect its articulations to have a place in an artificial language. *Does pure interactivity exist in the ordinary life-world?*

It is important to understand the principles that govern the shift from (1) to (2), and to further explore them. One of the most important of these principles is that education can never be perceived as a one-to-one relationship, not even in cases of a very private and personal contact between teacher and student, or parent and child. The fact that education transcends such individual relations directs us to what is normally indicated as the *setting* or the *context* of education. However, there is more to consider in emphasizing interactivity as a major principle in education. *Context* exceeds the pure surroundings of the education process, the classroom or the family. Context is an educational feature in its own right. If one renames this context, the issue becomes clearer. The context in an educational process is in essence its constituting *environment*. One can *construct such environments* with e-devices, and give them a particular function, for instance to stimulate and enhance the student's attention, involvement, and awareness in educational settings. As a consequence, we have to focus on a 'learning society' as the almost natural milieu for future forms of education that are aware of the implicit structure of communication.

That milieu does not take communication as a natural phenomenon. 'Growth' and 'learning' are complementary and therefore the most important building blocks in education. They also fit recent interpretations of society as *a learning society*—a concept that should be distinct from the concepts 'life-long learning' or 'permanent education'. The latter are too much concentrated on the individual as a fixed point of reference for social formation, and the suggestions about 'life-long' and 'permanent' do (again) not involve patterns of interactivity. That language focuses on *individuals,* which are *assisted* by continuously revised and reconsidered knowledge for sustaining a set of basic life conditions. This struggle for life is in no way compatible with any of the goals of modern education. A learning society is a society in which citizens are enabled to learn new ways of life, to adapt to new techniques and to understand new insights, and is a society that evaluates this type of citizenship positively.

Learning in a Learning Society

Our explanations of interactivity presuppose that students are always already embedded in today's culture and that they experience the influence of social and institutional contexts at any moment of their identity formation. The same is true for citizens, who were—after all—children and students before being considered citizens! Identity formation is at stake in the processes of interactivity for which education has to prepare them. Transfer of information and interactive training in basic structures of society constitute *challenges to change*—a change which does not exclude, but rather deepens, meanings and opinions in anterior phases of life.

There is no acquiring of any knowledge as if that happens for the first time in life; in other words: identity formation does not know an *ab ovo* situation! *Education does not concern the world as it is, but pertains to a world in change.* That is indeed a great challenge to the underlying structures of communication. To educate is to enter a process of change, and to contribute to—often to manage—that change. Assigned knowledge, information, and skills *change* existing patterns. The "newness" of that information and skills evaporates in the change itself. Any test, exam, or diploma guarantees how this accomplishment *once took place*—no more than that. A diploma is never a comfortable chair to doze in for a lifetime. Learning takes place *in* patterns of interactivity and must also be characterized *as* a form of communication that fits interactivity.

Learning in E-education

Modern education must organize education, training and skill-development in accordance with such insights. A few issues can be precisely defined and show the paradigmatic difference with the traditional understanding of the meaning of education:

1. "Learning as an element of electronic education" surpasses the pure transfer of knowledge, conceptual training, and elaboration of skills.

2. "Learning as an element of electronic education" contains more than the traditional programs of universities, training centers, or schools offer. The learning process is a life-long event, and covers all fundamental aspects of modern life.

3. "Learning as an element of electronic education" transcends the limited goals of a single social function, role, or diploma. All learning processes contribute to social change—a change that continues to occur through individuals that change the change;

4. "Learning as an element of electronic education" always reaches beyond traditional understandings of education;

5. "Learning as an element of electronic education" in this sense of the word concerns its students in every aspect of their life cycle. That type of learning must validate the principle that *to educate is to respect Human Rights.*

This is particularly true in new developments of e-education, and its focus on interactivity. Recent multimedia techniques and e-educative programs bring that issue to the fore. Is the "new student" in danger of becoming a part of his or her laptop? This question reflects again a conservative view on education, with the student as receiver and the educator as sender of information and training instructions. This archaic sender-receiver pattern should no longer function as the basis of our understanding of communication. Education is the field of experience, in which that pattern is invalidated in practice as well as in theory. Today's reality is different. Four aspects of e-education show this important and fascinating difference. They pertain to: (a) the place and function of electronic devices; (b) the seductive character of those devices, in particular the computer; (c) the indeterminacy of knowledge involved; and (d) the mediating power of electronic devices.

The quality of behaviors and social communication influences the students to perceive an electronic education context as *fascinating*, with instructors who transcend the pure reproductive dimensions of traditional education and communication. They experience how *living together is learning together.* Learning processes much more than the simple mechanism of accounting duties; they pertain to an involvement in ongoing social and personal change. *To learn is to change, and to change is to learn.* Such understanding invalidates the geometry that once provided our traditional basis for interaction as a major form of living together. 'Change', in the context of electronic education and its predominant forms of communication should become a major catchword.

CHAPTER II

INTERACTIVITY PHILOSOPHICALLY

§ 1 Introduction

Electronically enhanced education, or E-education, is a contradictory expression in as far as its history is concerned. All emphasis on the electronic component seems to relate to the *short* history of electronics in Western society. However, if one stresses the education component, then it appears that its history is as *long* as Western culture. Think of Ancient Greek ideas (which never existed without references to pedagogy) or modern critical viewpoints in pedagogy, social sciences or a philosophy of 'Deconstruction' in the sense of Jacques Derrida.

The combination of the two is bewildering. The few decades of electronics combined with the millennia of education creates a feeling of ambiguity. That ambiguity is reinforced by the fact that electronics suggest an almost natural predominance of *technical* development and know-how. But is the 'history' of electronic knowledge and technical know-how really a 'history' in the sense of our daily language and also our common ideas on education?

References to the common good in society or to other basic values and norms of society look in essays on the history of electronics like a *corpus alienum*. Yet, the two types of history, the extremely long one and the very short one, have shared ideas, insights, and principles—an idea that is fascinating, and deepens the basics of e-education as well.

This comes in particular to the fore if one highlights some principles at work in E-education, which were not part of Ancient Greek, Roman, or Christian traditions, but rather show Hebraic themes in effect. There are two introductory issues.

First is what the preceding chapter explained as "a turn in understanding communication": the turn from communication engendered by an

autonomous individual towards communication as an element of an unfolding personality with awareness about the implicated other as a basis for any
human identity. That is the basis for any thought formation in the field of electronic education as a special case of e-communication.

Secondly, we highlight a sentence from the preceding chapter which formulated how *any ego-centered communication is a linear communication,* often represented by the concept of "interaction", for instance between an ego and an alter
ego. The turn towards the presence of an *alter ego* in each developing *ego* is a
form of dialectics, which is central in the practice of electronic communication,
and opens new attitudes in education in general. These issues come up with a
further exploration of specifically Hebrew motives in the heart of German
Idealism at the end of the 19th century in Central Europe. The movement
received another name, which quickly became subject of criticism and disap-
proval: "The German Jewish Renaissance".

§ 2 The German-Jewish Renaissance

Arthur A. Cohen mentions the "German-Jewish Renaissance" in his 1962 book[xvii] as if this Renaissance were an established historical fact. There are, however, arguments not to use this name, not only because of the emotional contents of the expression "German-Jewish" (itself not unlike like 'Christian-Jewish'), but also because of negative connotations of 'Renaissance' or 'Enlightenment' in the spiritual life of modernity. And last but not least: this Renaissance was Jewish although it took place on German soil and appeared to be vital for German thinkers. The expression is understandable in so far as the word "Renaissance" remained an indication for the entirety of post-Middle Age thinking for many non-Jewish thinkers.

However, this Renaissance refers to the self-interpretation and self-awareness of Jews and German culture in Central Europe. It remains an issue of the cultural history of Europe and is not a matter of Jewish religion. The word 'Renaissance' has a specific meaning: "finding your identity anew". It thus refers to evaluating your history. In doing just that, traditions are kept alive. But an identity is never created *ab ovo,* rather in *repetition*. Repetitions are parallels that function in the pattern of culture and consciousness.

A detailed representation of the German-Jewish ties in the case of the central issue at stake is in Jürgen Habermas' 1961 publication *Der Deutsche Idealismus der Jüdischen Philosophen*. This title shows a perspective together with specific lines of determination. Jewish philosophers used and expressed basic ideas of German Idealism, especially the substance of what we called "the turn in understanding communication", or "the practice of dialectics in communication". But that project has ultimately little to do with Jewish philosophy. We are warned by Habermas, a German sociologist and philosopher, that the theme contains not a simple registration of facts and constellations, but is rather a focus point of Occidental thinking, whereby a farewell to our extreme individualisms remains the major issue.

The concept of "the German-Jewish Renaissance" (expression used by Arthur Cohen) can be compared with a parallel concept in Habermas' philosophical and historical views. The question comes up, whether German thinkers as well as Jewish have been fascinated by Romanticism, Mysticism, Metaphysics—and in what regard those mainstreams of thought in the minds of the two types of authors were compatible enough to form a coherent substance with a specific historic indication. In any case, we have to have a minimal awareness of the problems involved.

A number of conceptual approaches imply an interpretation of the relations between German and Jewish philosophers. There is the German "Verständigung"(coming to terms) and the emphasis of the encompassing history of ideas: "Geistesgeschichte". There is, furthermore, Walter Benjamin's suggestion that all this is a matter of "*constellations*", a concept he borrowed from astronomy and astrology. Today, we would speak of a "German-Jewish connection". We would formulate with more caution that there is a "*dialogue constellation*"—a dialogue being the expression for the essence of the contrast between Occidental individualism and Jewish emphasis on the almost sacred duality of life.

However, one should not only concentrate on the name that we use in connection with a presentation of the content we envisage. It remains thereby important that German and Jewish thinking (and not for example French or Spanish, who were also very close with Jewish thought, but in a different mood) had an equal intensity of mystic and metaphysic experiences. It shows how there is a form of human life possible which transcends the borderlines of being Jewish or German, the lines between the "natural and the non-natural Jew", as Cohen states.

But that is not enough. There is not only a transgression of Jewish/German features but rather an *integrating transgression* which makes racial and cultural properties dissipate in order to reach another, perhaps higher, level. That's really dialectics in the sense of Hegel, and the emergence of new possibilities in individual and cultural life. The privileges of experiencing such states of mind are always historical and thus transcending any individual road to identity. And experience is inherent to that road, so that one must focus the appropriate *social* dimensions of communication.

§ 3 Buber and Rosenzweig

Franz Rosenzweig (1886–1929) and Martin Buber (1878–1965) acquired world fame, integrated the rich Jewish tradition of philosophies and narratives, and influenced their contemporaries far beyond the boundaries of strict Hebraic thoughts in Western culture.

Their special attention was to shape Jewish education, and actively participate in it, spiritually as well as institutionally. They were enormously important figures of cultural transition, and encountered Hegel, Schelling and Hölderlin as major determinants in their uniquely productive Tübingen period. They honored earlier philosophical achievements, which preceded their insights, and took those as their own concern. For instance, H. Jacobi formulated in 1775 the unity of *I* and *Thou* as a fundamental viewpoint: "I open eyes and ears, or I extend my hand and feel in that moment how inseparable they are: I and Thou, Thou and I."

Ludwig Feuerbach mentioned how philosophical Idealism was wrong when it strove to understand the *I* without a sensed *Thou* (§41)[xviii]. He opened the gates for new conceptions of reality and of social life, forming a sound prelude to existentialism (Jaspers, Heidegger, Marcel, Sartre), phenomenology (Husserl) and philosophical anthropology (Scheler, Pleßner, Gehlen), three philosophical mainstreams of the first decades of the 20th century.

What was a spiritual reality became also a political reality: Buber's opinion was more than once sought in the first days of the State of Israel. One should not forget his central role in a period of ideological conflict, especially with Nazism and the consequences of the Holocaust, which appeared to be a hinge of Western culture.

Three Principles

Three principles are essential in the profiling of approaches and methodologies in preliminary off-computer educative stages as well as in full-fledged computer related E-education situations. A confrontation with them leads to the described turn in our understanding of communication, particularly in electronic communication.

The *first* principle is that *E-education is an institutional activity* and never just a person to person, or person to electronic device relationship. One should understand E-education as truly education and emphasize therefore the exquisite quality of the parent-children as well as the teacher-student association. This principle gives ample attention to the archetypical connection between father and son, to which Hebraic traditions have to say fresh and for our society surprisingly new words.

It is as if the described renewal of human relations by means of modern genetics was already foreseen in those traditions. They are indeed far beyond our socially fashionable individualism and pragmatism or the nearly polytheist Christian understanding of that connection. None of these aspects discredits or obliterates the importance of E-education as a new and specific, even a central *institutional* feature in social life. Their institutional embedding is the school as well as the family—hardly without a noticeable difference between the two.

The *second* principle is in the fundamental function of the *dialogue* and of dialogic approaches of social issues—not in the least important issues in education. Franz Rosenzweig is an outstanding exponent of the emphasis on dialogue in the beginning of the 20th century, which brought German philosophers and "Jewish thinkers" (often positioned beyond broader philosophical concerns) together. He and Martin Buber reshaped the dialogic position in ways that became important in our next century.

New experiences and new forms of dialogic life came into existence with electronic communication by the pressure of newly drawn borderlines between real and virtual communication. This makes E-education an outstanding field for new social experiences that need the compass of a rigorously reshaped structure of dialogue. A sharp contrast exists between this new thinking and education as limited to data transfer, to information and learning.

The *third* principle for E-education is the unfolding of radical *respect* between the participants in educative relationships. This principle reaches beyond the achievement of respect from balancing interests of single individuals. It is also beyond the reach and understanding of a strictly formalized legal discourse: respect is neither in the perfect equilibrium of interests, nor in the outbalancing of subject-positions in society.

Education has to achieve more than just training in individual give-and-take status or the balance of individual rights to form the common good in society. It's interesting in this perspective that virtual scenes in E-education are no longer compatible with such thought patterns. There is no reliable connection between the world of electronic images and communications on the one hand and the life-world based in a concept of the common good that results from the arithmetic of individual interests.

Respect nourishes and fulfils the life of individuals and is clearly not the result of negotiation, but rather a condition to participate in education as aiming at an individual's *becoming*. Goals and standards of that becoming are not pragmatically engendered by authorities or institutions, but by an enhanced self-understanding pertaining to one's own role in democracy. Emphasis is therefore on E-education as a particular environment, often shaped high-tech in a technological as well as a social sense of the word. It therefore requires *interactivity* between all participants in that environment *as a source for respect*. Whilst fulfilling this requirement, E-education enhances the self-understanding of individuals in the context of socialization.

Rosenzweig on Institutions

Franz Rosenzweig is, with Martin Buber and Abraham Heschel, one of the most widely read Jewish thinkers in Western Europe. He expresses the strong desire to reconnect the profound truths of Judaism with the lives of ordinary people—Jews and non-Jews alike. An assimilated Jew and scholar of German philosophy, Rosenzweig was on the point of conversion to Christianity when the experience of a Yom Kippur service during WW I in 1913 brought him back to Judaism, and he began to study with the philosopher Hermann Cohen.

Seeking how to be an observant Jew in the modern world, Rosenzweig refused to characterize the traditions of Jewish law as mere rituals, customs, and folkways. His aim was to find Judaism by living it, and to live it by knowing it more deeply. In his books, papers and public addresses, we find important stimuli to engage in new forms of thinking, reading, and listening as well as specific indications of how to understand education in this framework of philosophical positions.

His correspondence with Buber especially discloses some of the most important features regarding the essence of education in its relation to institutions. The letters were mainly written in the years from 1920, when Rosenzweig considered his wishes as "the messengers of trust" through 1922, when he took action to install "Das Freie Jüdische Lehrhaus" in Frankfurt am Main. The English name "Free Jewish House of Study" is a translation of Nahum Glatzer, who translated the expression "Lehrhaus" as "New Jewish Studies Center".

Establishing this institution was extremely important in promoting new ways of learning and education. The following aspects were particularly outstanding:

(a) *A "Lehrhaus" differs from a "Volkshochschule"*, a "People's Academy", in those days in Germany a new move in the democratization process of education. The names indicate contrasting convictions. The "Volkshochschule" seemed only a different version of German academic life and its bourgeois hierarchy of civil relations. That "…in our case meaningless word 'Volk' should be replaced…but 'Society for Jewish Education' would hardly do", Rosenzweig formulated in a letter to Rudolf Hallo in December 1922[xix].

The 'Lehrhaus' had to become a modern *Beth ha Midrash* and by no means a new University. Notice that in the same year, Rosenzweig was offered a chair at the Frankfurt University for Jewish Religion and Ethics, which was, due to Rosenzweig's illness, occupied by Buber in 1924. However, the 'Lehrhaus' was and should be a place for discussion and mutual learning, not just for representing scientific authority.

(b) The new learning goes with *a new appreciation and interpretation of language*. To understand the essence of language is to approach the central importance of education as a process of *becoming, growth,* and being *cultured*. Language is an institutional fact—an observation that Rosenzweig proclaimed to have made as an important step in the direction of understanding the close ties between education and language teaching, the latter being a form of language acquisition.

"My point of departure is here, that there is ultimately only one language; each language contains potentially—even in dialects and infantile languages— all other languages of humanity" he writes to Hallo. He adds: "This is why I can gain from my German throat and soul all Hebrew 'rules' through understanding and interpretation."

(c) *Language is the milieu of all education*. The destruction of the good taste of a Hebrew text may result from grammatical analysis. Only a repeated reading could restore this. When introducing the idea of a Jewish Lehrhaus, Rosenzweig again connects the essence of the Jewish character and the act of reading.

In his 1920 essay *Bildung und kein Ende* (On Education) he says: "It is something inside the individual that makes him a Jew, something infinitesimally small yet immeasurably large, his most impenetrable secret, yet evident in every gesture and every word—especially in the most spontaneous of them. The Jewishness I mean is no 'literature'. It can be grasped through neither the writing nor the reading of books. It is only lived—and perhaps not even that. One *is* it."

And here is more to say[xx]. "Hebrew, knowing no word for "reading" that does not mean "learning" as well (and 'learning' is here 'educating', not 'instructing' or 'training'!), has given this, the secret of all literature, away. For it is a secret, though a quite open one, to these times of ours—obsessed and suffocated as they are by education—that books exist only to transmit that which has been achieved to those who are still developing. While that which is between the achieved and the developing, that which exists today, at this moment—life itself—needs no books. If I myself exist, why ask for something to 'educate' me? But children come and ask; and the child in myself awakes— the child that doesn't as yet 'exist' and doesn't 'live'—and it asks and wants to be educated and to develop—into what? Into something living, into something that exists. But just here is where an end is put to the making of books".

So "there is no end to learning (in the sense of 'education'), no end to education. Between these two burns the flame of the day, nourished by the limited fuel of the moment: but without its fire the future would remain sealed and without its illumination the past would remain invisible." History of humans and the institutions in life are forged together by a never-ending education.

One particular aspect of the complex institutional situation in Rosenzweig's case should be highlighted, his lingering attachment to Germany, and its profound effect on his conception of Judaism. This issue must be addressed if we want to take his thought seriously and not merely preserve him as one more exhibit in a museum of Weimar culture.

A substantial detail of this constellation is in the question of whether Rosenzweig's thoughts can be separated from his realistic struggle to create an institution to educating in the lines of his thoughts.

(d) *Not only language but also speaking is an institutional issue.* Rosenzweig cherished a 'discussion room' as the center of a school or 'Lehrhaus'. He describes the innermost function of language by observing the institutional framework of *talking*—and its architecture. That clarifies how institutions sustain the effect and force of education.

This is the more important for E-education institutions because there are not only teachers and participants, but also computers, programs, and E-devices creating essential messages and teachings among all participants. One needs to approach all these persons and issues not by way of force, contract, or other legal obligation but by the way of *respect* and *trust*.

All this characterizes Rosenzweig's words, written long before the e-communication hype of today: "Have 'confidence' for once. Renounce all plans. To begin with, don't offer them anything. Listen. And words will come to the listener, and they will join together and form desires. And desires are the messengers of confidence. The teacher able to satisfy such spontaneous desires cannot be a teacher according to a plan; he must be much more and much less, a master and at the same time a pupil. It will not be enough that he himself knows or that he himself can teach. He must be capable of something quite different— he himself must be able to 'desire'. He who can desire must be the teacher here".

Those sentences do not only characterize an educational attitude, which embraces the principles bearing fruit from their Hebraic roots. They are also deeply psychological, as if metaphysical motives come to light that determine an image of man in a culture that transcends possessive individualism.

These words describe precisely the necessary skills and attitude of today's teachers in E-education. The ability to respect, to wait, to awaken desire in students and the teacher himself reflects in his or her ability to talk to the students. It might be surprising that conversational skills are of utmost importance in the setting of E-education—it is not the electronics but the talking and the language mastering that makes the E-educator successful. The same is true for the architecture of the 'Lehrhaus' (in Rosenzweig's case) and the E-education Centers (in the case of contemporary E-education).

Teachers

The qualities of the teachers are not reflected in plans or diplomas, but in their position (physically and psychologically) in the spatial dimensions of speech. To say the same in a less philosophical terminology: the teachers must constantly *become* teachers, and never solely *be* teachers. The difference between becoming and being characterizes the necessary attitude in E-educational settings. It is again Rosenzweig who, in outlining his ideas on education in the Frankfurt 'Lehrhaus', brought architecture, social hierarchy, and teaching together in one space, which he called the 'discussion room'.

The emphasis on such a room emphasizes the institutional character of speech. "The teachers will be discovered in the same discussion room and the same discussion period as the students. And in the same discussion hour the same person may be heard as both master and student. In fact, only when this happens will it become certain that a person is qualified to teach."

There exist no rooms in a 'Lehrhaus' and in E-education Centers, which do not sustain the process of *becoming*. This is a criterion that should be accepted by all those who pretend to live in a house where children and inmates can simply not avoid educating each other.

Houses where people live together are humming spots where conversations never end. Today, those conversations do not exclusively contain spoken words, but also conversations often interwoven with fragments of writing, e-mails, notes and other e-communication techniques. The idea of an architectural unity that protects these scenes of communicative humming is in the concept of a common room. "It is essential that the discussion place be a single room—without a waiting room. The discussion must be 'public'. Those who come can wait in the discussion room itself. They can wait until the moment comes for them to join in. The discussion should become a conversation. Anyone who wants to continue the conversation with a single person can make an appointment for some later time. The discussion period should bring everybody together. For it brings people to each other on the basis of what they all have in common. There has been enough of speechmaking. The speaker's platform has been perverted into a false pulpit long enough. The voices of those who want these desirous students to desire them as teachers must lose the 'true ring' of dead-sure conviction"[xxi]

The "principle of indeterminacy" does not only play a role in computer-related education settings. Indeed, indeterminacy inhabits the computer. But it seems also important for conversations, because speech acts and talking in general can be delete know the indeterminate as well.

Are words of the other person not by definition undetermined in meaning and articulation, and never in total conformity with our expectations? The risk that a teacher expresses unexpected opinions and comes up with out-of-the-box articulations is a risk each student has to cope with—it is a structure that determines the risk of the teacher in view of the student as well. Is conversation, e-communication included, solely a matter of risk-taking, or its opposite, the avoidance of risks?

Do not forget how Rosenzweig emphasized that the 'conversation room' in the 'Lehrhaus' should be *a public place*. The public character of that place diminishes the risks in mutual talk, he must have thought.

Today, probably as a result of widespread e-communication intertwining with our conversations, the risks may remain the same but the separation between public and private spaces is less clear than ever. The concepts of public and private have to be redefined, even in legal discourse. The relevance of that distinction changes with the different practices to manage the separation in times of omnipresent e-conversations or genetic consult, which is also unthinkable without computers delivering statistics.

These inspirations show *new* dimensions for education in general and E-education in particular. One should recognize how Western education possesses a two-sided face. We always educate, train, and teach as matter of self-expression and also as an indication of the self-interpretation of our selves, touching time and being in their metaphysical relevance. All self-expression is a form of esthetics: through education we give form to life and our world beyond the generation gaps.

Self-interpretation is a form of existential responsibility: through education we mirror our selves in confrontation with our history and beliefs. This mirroring should not be neglected because of our addiction to electronic communications with their potential to change realities and their power of dominance in human communication.

Buber on Dialogue

There are striking similarities and a deep harmony between the position of Rosenzweig in his major work *The Star of Redemption* (1921) and Buber in his world famous *I and Thou* (1923), both already readable from in 1922. A central point of convergence is in the new interpretation and function of the *dialogue*. It is especially Buber who has drawn attention to the dialogue. And it is fully understandable that our modern interest in that theme is interrelated with all manifestations of electronic communication, including education. The dialogue was, in Hebrew thinking, a place of renewal of religious and social relations, a structure of anthropological importance, and a fresh motive for social and psychological approaches to man in Western society.

Those reflections became even more important through the extension of electronics in human communication. That new aspect was not foreseeable in Buber's time. None of those authors, however, would have been astonished or feel the need to revise his theory because of the appearance of electronic communication.

In the same period of renewed interest in the dialogue, Gershom Sholem researched Jewish Mysticism and the Kabbalah as well as Chassidism—a theme also exploited by Buber. Close friend to Rosenzweig, Buber, and Benjamin, he laid the groundwork for an academically recognized scientific discipline[xxii] named *Comparative Religion.*

The dialogue structure also remained of essence in these studies. The word 'Mysticism' in his book's title was written to make the publication accessible for the general public, although his real theme was Gnosticism, and his new scientific approach (not unlike Schelling's) was the study of *stories and histories in images.* He could use this tactic, because, after all, dialogues represent images! Buber's multiple writings on the Chassidism had stimulated the same insight.

This clarifies how *foundational texts on dialogue were not just emerging from a renewed interest in social sciences or psychology.* A dialogue appears to be a cornerstone of social life, a nucleus of personality development. Buber knew Freud and had read many of his writings. Did Freud sufficiently notice? One often reads how his exposure of the dialogue resulted from social and psychological interests, and Buber's writings on the Chassidism were interpreted in the perspective of those interests. That is, however, a shortsighted interpretation[xxiii].

The unfolding of studies pertaining to the dialogic nature of humankind were not solely rooted in an interest in social studies but in religion—as was the case of Scholem's interest in Gnosticism. Buber's *I and Thou* had grown out of his lectures *Religion as Presence*, given January/March 1922 at Rosenzweig's *Freies Jüdisches Lehrhaus* in Frankfurt. Why is this confluence important to us? Does it not happen often that lectures give birth to books that later become world famous?

Buber's *I and Thou* had its spiritual source in *educational relations* and its institutional framework, the 'Lehrhaus', which is an *educational* setting. The 'Lehrhaus' as an institution was at great distance from the Frankfurt University and not identifiable with any other "Academy of the Science of Judaism" found elsewhere in Germany. And notice how the 'Lehrhaus' was the ideal institutional context for exposing the core issue in terms of *I—Thou* versus *I—It* relations.

It was *not* the institution to talk and demonstrate authority, but the golden opportunity to discuss, to share thoughts and venture an exchange of ideas beyond speaking, writing and publishing—in short, a new approach to education and its methods for enriching its participants. The principle is clearly anchored in the Hebrew tradition: words refer to worlds and the words of a single person therefore need numerous living others.

Again: What importance should we give to this specific constellation? If no reading of a word is without reference to education, then the most favorable milieu for reading is only in an educational institution. But this observation is not rooted in social or psychological understandings.

Education always requires a *metaphysical* foundation. Rosenzweig highlights this insight in an essay on the new format of thinking he developed, and characterizes Buber's *I and Thou* as a book "in which the author, who has something new to say, can use old Jewish words. Jewish issues are, like all issues, always bygone; Jewish words are, however, although old, part of the eternal youth of the word, and renew the world when invited to enter "[xxiv].

Two important dimensions are in Buber's lectures on "*Religion as Presence*": they are *Time*, and *Reality*. *Time* is in the *immediacy* that makes encounters possible and lends them their value. *Reality* is in acknowledging that all spiritual and material existence is grounded in *encountering*. Time and reality constitute a double face—a face to be recognized by all of us, a process deeply influenced by "being together" as an educative exigency. One side of that face is determined by what we already experienced in life, our history, the many paths we already walked. The other side is the mark of our confrontation with the other, his or her, being that gives us the possibility of experiencing the wholeness and complete reality of our life.

Buber formulated: "Jedes wirkliche Geschehen des Geistes ist Begegnung, und dieses vor allem, ein Ausgehen und Begegnen". An encounter is never an act on its own. Each fragment of spiritual befalling is a form of meeting, its dynamics are found in *Exodus* and *Encounter*. Reality is in two parts, one half and another half, one could say. A part is mine, and a part is yours—that is the fascination of *I and Thou*.

It was already the basic conviction of Immanuel Kant, who explained in his 1795 anti-war essay *Zum Ewigen Frieden* (On Perpetual Peace) how hospitality is a necessary condition for being a person worth the high esteem of others. Only one who reaches out can take in. Hospitality is one of the two forces that meet, beyond any artificially acquired passivity, receptivity, social conditioning or psychological reinforcement.

Buber qualifies the meeting of *I* and *Thou* in its dependence on the *I* as well as on the *Thou* and especially the oncoming of the *Thou* a "Revelation", thus indicating how metaphysics always intertwines with religion. Reality is more than any representation can achieve. That viewpoint is at a distance from a neo-capitalist society and its liberal philosophy.

Dialogue is not an arbitrary element of social life, but its metaphysical ground-work—no wonder that education is needed to enable social life to achieve and reinforce its form and shape.

§ 4 Words and Worlds

Hebrew language is given a special appreciation in view of experiencing the world and educating for entering life. Words are germs, they are algorithms, and they contain complex meanings and access many interpretations of reality. There is a firm correlation between word and world. What words imply tells about how the world is. Buber concentrated on three words, which are not particular Hebrew, but he treated them the Hebrew way! These words are: *I, Thou* and *It*. Three words, three worlds, which are One, but the Oneness is hidden in the relations between the three.

His many conferences and texts gave priority to the *I—Thou* relationships. This is also the case when discussing and corresponding with Rosenzweig, not to mention many others. *I* and *Thou* are Cherut, an experienced path, a vivid presence, presence like a vertical, a hazardous undertaking to bridge the *I* and the *non—I*, to play the game of identity and non-identity. The world as it is, and humans as they are, seem twofold: one and one. They are only one is as far they are not one, but this *and* of one and one. However, do not forget that this approach results from the use of *words* whereby even the experience of one's own identity of the 'I' is marked by a linguistic articulation.

Western thought understands this as an act of reproduction, in philosophical terminology: *representation*. It means that words mirror reality in a one-to-one relationship. The Hebrew tradition emphasizes, however, that words lay foundations, constitute relations, and are not a reality *per se,* but rather create reality. According to Buber, that contrast also characterizes an educational relationship.

If an educator represents traditions, as he mostly does in the Western tradition, he represents secure values and norms and a stable set of knowledge. His secured knowledge precedes the knowledge of all students and forms the basis for all educational relationships. Transference of that knowledge gives him a solid social position, including the respect of his students and society at large. Doubts about his position and indeterminacy pertaining to his knowledge would immediately diminish such an educational relation.

But that attitude is incompatible with E-education. In E-education, transference does not pertain to secured knowledge from which a social position is deduced. There is an important point of departure here. Any E-teacher is, together with his student, in a situation of search and discovery. They exploit a totally different attitude. Teacher and student must be open to all possibilities that e-communication offers—the information knowledge of the Internet with the indeterminacy of e-devices and computers included.

Any *I—Thou* relation as envisaged by Buber flourishes in contacts with the world of E-, its computers, Internet provisions, programs, and virtual reality included. It is because that relation includes immediacy between the partners, and finds its base in a common interest, namely psychological openness of all participants towards the unknown dimensions of meaning and knowledge. Do not forget that a computer always knows more than any of its users knows.

Buber teaches us[xxv] that *what is spoken, needs the other*. Computers participate in the constitution of the Otherness of all participants in manners never seen or experienced before! E-communication and E-education understand Buber's teaching as their foundation: each communication needs the other, not as the receiver of what had been sent, but as the foundation of the communication itself. This could be interpreted as one of the most challenging aspects of the emergence of the E-world and, for instance, virtual reality.

Those considerations show that Hebraic traditions and thoughts and E-education might be deeply compatible. Such compatibility cannot be found in traditional Western education. Hence the general feeling that the E-world is alien to EDUCATION and only forwards the use of electronics in LEARNING processes—and that is precisely *not* the case!

All that unfolds another aspect of Buber's explorations of the *dialogue*. It is necessary to understand that his analyses of the dialogue and their far-reaching consequences are apparently *structural*. In other words, the *dialogue* in Buber's writings indicates *positions* between participants of conversation and discourse. He thus uses expressions like 'attitude', 'spirit', 'disposition', or 'foundation', for instance when he concludes: *"who says 'You' does not say anything"*.

The utterance does not describe or *represent*, as would have been the outcome with Kant or Descartes, but *creates* the reality that *You are You by means of the utterance of the word itself*. Here is again the opposition between Roman and Hebrew traditions, between *representation* and *creation* as the germ of the world. It leads to subtle distinctions, to a form of mapping of utterances, which are directly related to words in conversation or even written in texts.

A starting point is not a substance, but a relation—just as electronic communication teaches us. There is the *I*, but the *I* is nothing, that is: not-a-thing. The *I* is always either from an *I—Thou* or an *I—It* relationship. These two are two *worlds*, and the *I* just exists in both. That coincidence does not imply any ground for the emphasis Western thought gives to the *I* as a privileged subject.

Two *Worlds* and just one *I*—where is the virtual, and where the real? These might change in accordance to the coordinates that build the constellation: they may be *You* as well as *It*, but only insofar as the *You* belongs to an *I—Thou* world, although the *You* could also have its home in the *I—It* world. Now an essential question arises, which has hitherto never been considered in the literature about the dialogic principle. Does the world of electronic devices and communication, virtual realities included, belong to the *It—*world, so that students in E-education, like all computer users, are by definition in the *I—It* world, or do they belong to the *I—Thou* world?

Philosophers of modern Western culture tend to answer the question by referring to the qualities of the *It*-world. This is in line with theories that interpret e-communication and other practices of e-devices as an alienation phenomenon. Others, who step outside of those boundaries and often view the recent e-phenomena more positively on the basis of their own experiences with e-communicative contexts, will not join this value judgment.

Let's reformulate the complicated issue at stake. The ultimate question is about the *I* of electronic communications, including Internet, Virtual Reality and E-education. Is this *I* a component of the *I—Thou* world or of the *I—It* world, Buber made us question. The two are, in his opinion, very different, because the first is based on immediacy and naturalness, whereas the second embraces the opposite. But our e-technology taught us that that all immediacy is mediated, often by unknown and metaphysical means.

Where mediation appears, the discussion about naturalness follows. The naturalness of the *I—Thou* world is a naturalness that differs from the *I—It* world. One should label it *artificial naturalness*. The boundaries between the two worlds are no more than a degree of artificiality. Artifice is a major feature of culture and the human mind. The "pure" naturalness is a thought, an ideology, and thus an artifice of the human mind, Buber could already have noticed.

But he did not, and only our contemporaries, puzzled and fascinated by E-realities, experienced the many degrees of artificiality, which intrude on the multiple practices of human life. And this is what happens in E-education. Its subjects are for Buber and the Hebrew tradition *an I that lives the It—WORLD as if it was a THOU-WORLD*: ask the students in their context of E-devices with its education programs, and they will tell you! That insight makes their actions understandable. They perform long conversations with their fingers, at times beyond the social norms for each other's accessibility.

All writing and its words are products of knowledge and education, language acquisition, and a feeling for grammar and syntax, which is automatically sustained and corrected by the spell checkers in their computer. They write and switch off their mastering of the language. Reading happens with letters and images: a new ideogrammatic consciousness. Their word games are translations of world games in their mind.

A new world becomes articulated, a world based on degrees of artificiality. There is no fear anymore to dissolve its foundation in acts that *represent*. Recognizing the artifice is a matter of honoring the Presence—hence Buber's approach to Religion as Presence instead of the Idolatry of a Represented. The E· of E-education does not disturb, but rather enriches the relations with the *It-world*. And there is no sign of alienation anymore. How can one explain this?

Buber translated Kant "On Hospitality", one could say. Hospitality, which Kant introduced as a basis for social relations, became language. Words need other persons, not to receive what a speaker sends, but to accomplish speech and discourse. Linguistic expressiveness does not exist without the presence of others. Our articulation is not solely our will and intention, but primarily a gift of others.

That is the clue to understanding how words can contain a world. It is the world that consists of other human beings, a social world, which plays its major role here—and not the physical world standing apart from human life. And that social world is ordered according to the relations between the self and others, which we maintain on the basis of commonality.

Rosenzweig understood this more radically than Buber. He criticized that the *I* in the *I—It world* is not really *spoken*, as Buber suggests in *I and Thou*, §2.4 and 2.5, but only *thought* as an element of that relational pattern. The *I—It* world is therefore, in contrast to the *I—Thou* world, never really spoken but always a product of thoughts, of imagination, we would today say: a *virtual* reality. One of the most interesting leads in this context is the consideration that the *I-It* world is *not* a complexity, a world of relations like the *I—Thou* world, but rather a virtual entity composed of relations that are a mixture of existential and technical features[xxvi]. Here is a major issue that functions as a basis for the proposition that principles of Hebraic culture and thought patterns import our understanding and practices of E-education.

Buber also translated Kant 'On Respect'. Only a person can give and receive respect, and only persons can achieve self-realization if they accept being confronted with the world of moral laws and principles. Respect does not represent morality, but rather expresses how a person is open to moral issues and moral reasoning. The spirit of morals seems to belong to the self-consciousness of a person. In that regard, moral laws are fundamental to human existence, Kant concluded.

Respect is the way in which human individuals access morality, including cultural and religious differences. When they do so, they also create awareness about themselves. Any experience of respect means experiencing identity.

Two dimensions are important here. First, the existential receptiveness of morals is never a matter of pure legal rule following. If it were so, morals would have nothing to do with any of the qualities of human identity. Second, being open to morals as expressed in respect is essentially an interpersonal issue. It is difficult to imagine how respect as a property of one's own would truly be respect.

The phenomenon of respect is, in other words, the manifestation of the social character of human individuals, as Kant remarks in his *Groundwork to the Metaphysics of Morals* (1785) and his *Critique of Practical Reason* (1788).

In words used by Buber, one must acknowledge that *respect* belongs to the *I—Thou* world and is just a metaphor about relations or circumstances of the *I—It* world. That forms the point of departure for considerations about respect in E-education. It is clear that mutual respect between teacher and student is necessary at all levels and ages. But how do electronics influence and sustain the self-consciousness of teachers and students, and how does respect correlate with this changing context? One has often signaled the predominant framework of Western possessive individualism. That issue has been and still is a matter of sociological research. It did, however, never touch the changing qualities of self-consciousness created by electronic communication.

It's fascinating that the appearance of E-education urges the initiation of new investigations about this subject. Respect seems a matter of deep self-confrontation and self-awareness. It is Kant's insight that all manifestations of respect appeal to the social nature of an individual. Emphasis on the understanding of this social character is equally important in electronic communication. The interpretation of "social" has priority in this context, whereas one is inclined to restrict oneself to question the properties and technicalities of electronics. These dimensions in E-education show a contrast to the arithmetic of respect in a Western individualist society and its legal thought patterns that treat respect like justice. That is the point of debate. Why?

The key to the "why?" question is in the expression "arithmetic", which presupposes the possibility to calculate with neutral and equal entities. You can't perform math with indeterminate or ever-changing numbers or other elements. So, what are the calculable elements in Western possessive individualism and liberalism?

The answer is: *individuals*, but not individuals in all varieties of culture and life; they are individuals as citizens and, more absolutely, as bearers of rights and duties, as legal subjects, as embodiments of rights. Education in Western society has such subjects and their relations as its basic material; individual properties of students are respected because they have a right to be respected as bearers of rights. Balances of rights are taken care of, rights are subjected to political and social struggles, rights are divided equally and form a shield of protection—being a bearer of rights is an ultimate quality in social life. The balancing is an ultimate arithmetic.

It is relevant that Buber, asked around 1948 to give his impression about the legitimacy of a State of Israel, answered in terms of an enlarged 'Lehrhaus' and by no means an Israel as what he called a 'normal State'. If a person receives and gives respect, then the respect is materially concretized in rights and rightpositions, which are arithmetically calculated and safeguarded. This is the opposite of the spirit of a 'Lehrhaus'.

This strong tendency to equalize *respect* and *justice* is philosophically problematic. Respect needs in this thought pattern the absolute and abstract autonomy and inviolability of the individual. It means that there is no place for any consideration of how an individual can depend upon being open to morals and the contribution of others to one's constitution. If the framework of individualism considers any openness to other persons and other life, then it is on the basis of exchange, of equal proportion and equal share.

The arithmetic comes first in Western thought and politics. There reigns a concealed authority, which controls the balances and equalities, so that respect can appear as a major instrument to fulfill peace. That authority has a legal-political name, and is called the "rule of law". Disregarding respect is thus disregarding the balanced arithmetic of human relations. Kant appreciated the arithmetic but not how respect was construed without participation of other persons in context. One of the contexts that fascinated him was the education process. If young individuals are in that process, they have respect as a mediator towards self-awareness and self-realization. He did not, however, conclude that education is only successful if it goes *against* this arithmetic of individualism, just because it hinders the growth of the self through the process of respect.

He thus envisaged something that we badly need today, and most prominently in education. Buber's texts on education are one of the many examples. *Who is not able to clear a space for another person in his or her self, annihilates the necessary patterns of communication and relations in life.* That person will be living at too far a distance to morals, ethics, and other dimensions of growth, sharing and participating life-values, so that the network of social relations breaks down. Acquiring openness for respect as based on the presence of others appears to be the heart of all education.

This is today experienced not only in the realm of psychology or even psychopathology, but also in the E-dimensions of education. Students and educators will tell us how the network—always a network of social relations and on our computers only present in a new form—breaks down when sharing is not a result of education. It literally breaks down under our eyes at the screen of our computers!

E-education has the task and the skills to explain to its students how such a breakdown occurs and can be repaired. It thereby not only focuses the technicalities of e-communication. It should pay greatest attention to the basic structures of human growth and conduct, which fulfil the major role in this drama. One should thereby not forget how such occurrences have been an issue in Western culture from its beginning to modern times. No human individual can emerge in solitude and structure the self without metaphysics. .

CHAPTER III

INFORMATION AND EDUCATION

PART I: INFORMATION

§ 1 INTRODUCTION

Watching TV advertisements or reading them in the newspapers makes one inclined to bemoan the misuses of information in a society that once promoted information as the ultimate in modern democracy. To be informed about literally everything was a social value and a right in civil society. Do we still agree?

That question is not purely rhetoric. We are sometimes overwhelmed by the *un*informed situation in which people live: they only watch the Weather Channel or local TV stations, do not read journals, and are just interested in some issues within the neighborhood: thefts and car accidents rather than community works or cultural and political events. Their illiteracy is stunning, and the number of these people increases every day. Is that a flight that distances them from their position in public space, a disinterest in public issues, a concentration on a very private life with the smallest dimensions of context and milieu? Is the overwhelming stream of information causing a low tide of interest in any expanded awareness?

The "totally informed citizen" does not enhance or help realize our democracy. Social and political scientists, administrators, and government officials are hardly able to hide their disappointment in this regard. They mistakenly believe that 'well informed' also means 'well educated'. If this is not enough, they also have difficulty understanding that an 'informed actor' is by no means a 'responsible actor'. It seems to be a basic problem for civil society in the

Western world, a problem that ultimately puts education in perspective. Since most of the information sent and received is electronically transmitted, one must consider whether E-information needs E-education in order to be effective and to become a pillar of democracy. *Is information without the support of education meaningful at all?*

§ 2 Language

The use of language or the production of speech-acts (as philosophers often say, inspired by John Searle's theory) is rooted in the existence of other individuals. We understand our articulations as influenced by others only as a matter of receiving what was sent to us, and of reacting to it. Yet, we would agree that words solely spoken in a community are meaningful.

Nobody can deny that the meaning of what we say derives from others who share meanings with us even before our own utterances are produced. And nobody can minimize the enormous power of that social process and the language involved in it. Sharing does not diminish creativeness; it rather shows the intensity of one's own creativity being embedded in the activities of others. It also emphasizes the importance of others for the growth and articulation of one's so-called 'original' viewpoint. In fact, one can never be original on one's own, and in the solitude of oneself. Belonging to the same language group seems vital for the existence and function of linguistic utterances. Our words are just purely physical phenomena when we leave their social context out.

Do not forget that all meaning is a product of the human mind. Words would be spoken in vain without their context in culture, and in particular without culturing and educating in the realm of meaning and sense. Or, to put it differently, one must admit that any linguistic activity, in particular any exchange of words or other linguistic utterances, would be nothing without the continuous process of education in a culture.

The same is true for information. Each bit of information is anchored in values, norms, and expectations of a cultural pattern. The social and political importance of information increased and changed considerably at the moment when E-communication acquired global dimensions and became a multi-cultural phenomenon. Any formation of new social structures relates importantly to the character and quality of electronically transferred data. *But to manage and understand information, one needs social and individual skills.* This initial observation already emphasizes how information does not stand on its own as an isolated social issue.

Information has persons and institutions as a determining target. E-communication in that regard is not different from letter writing, which also is aimed at persons and institutions. But subjects who function as sender and receiver of electronic communication show new and often surprising technical properties and structures when compared to the traditional letter writing. However, electronic letters are still written with receivers in mind, and data are still produced with consumers in mind. The language in E-mails may differ from handwritten letters and even a specific electronic mail style might have been developed, but the structure of intentions remains the same, and so does the circulation in *public space.*

The relevance of E-education relates in surprising and sometimes bewildering ways to new public spaces. That can happen on a small scale in the heart of well-established communities, but also on a larger scale when companies or even states merge to form more extended supranational, normative, and economic units. This observation is equally relevant for cultures of enterprise as for state communities. It does not regard the geographical and physical dimensions in the first place, but rather the qualities of the new public spaces.

The major general issue remains that *new forms of information and communication require complementary forms of education.* It is not surprising, therefore, that recent developments in electronic communication and information require specially adapted forms of education, nowadays known as 'E-education'. This is the reason to further consider some of the basics of e-education.

§ 3 E-education

Every form or type of education is an indispensable process in shaping an individual's existence and engendering a personal identity. A cluster of traditional concepts such as training and preservation, self-control and self-reliance, instruction and learning, cultivation and culturing aim at an individual's *becoming*. To become a person, a civilized individual, a citizen is a culturally determined and a value-related expression pertaining to the *becoming* of a self. More than that—goals and standards of that becoming reflect society's self-understanding in its structures of representation in democracy.

E-education targets socialization like any other type of education. Social and individual values and viewpoints enable a person to share, to participate and to add extra value to the life of others (also called 'enhancement'). These norms and values assist students to become responsible citizens and to master the language of the institutions in which they must live their lives. Such an attitude about education demonstrates the general insight that *to educate is to change*. Change is most important in E-education. Principles of that change are reason, good faith, rationality, and respect for an individual's rights, experiences, feelings, and emotions in the unfolding of a person.

It might be bewildering that no mention has yet been made of the "E·"—component in the expression "E-education". This is because it should be emphasized from the very beginning that *education* is the focus of E-education, not education's *electronic devices*. And it also does not mean that E-education is solely "education *plus* electronics". Electronics are not just a new instrument in the context of education.

Our insight should become deeper and be more differentiated. The major difficulty in understanding the essence of E-education, which has students, teachers, and parents in its grip, pertains to the fact that the *E·* is not an additional tool for education, but that the *E·* changes everything involved in education. Reality and personality are changed, as well as knowledge and reflections. The entering of the *virtual* into public space (made possible via Internet café's, games, and other means) is an example of this observation. The *E·* is a symbol for education in a new key. The *E·* pertains to new and hitherto unknown levels of reality that need to be accepted and managed in education today.

It should therefore be emphasized again that E-education does not solely rely upon *one* specific electronic device (the computer) and *one* particular provision (Internet). E-education is a multi-media event. Virtually all E-devices can play a role in the theory and practice of E-education. These devices can be very different. Think of a camcorder, a video, a camera, a film, a walkman, a walkie-talkie, a computer program, a computer game, a game boy, a network of interactive programs, an environment where such programs are in-*built* devices, an entire video or TV studio, a wired classroom or any other specific E-center. All of these serve the broader purpose of education by means of e-instruments. If that purpose leads to the enhancement of skills and of changes in behaviors, then this is a matter of education, not of a pure application of E-devices.

There is consequently no exclusive focus on specific skills, techniques or know-how that relate only to specifically targeted electronic devices. The extremely wide range of E-educational relevance shows how E-education really pertains to a different world, and not to the world 'only' viewed differently. Again: E-education today sustains the implementation of an electronically accessed *reality*. Any definition of E-education would therefore interpret the *E·* not only as a symbol for electronically enhanced education, but rather as an all embracing symbol for a different world: a world with multiple meanings, unimagined techniques, hitherto unknown facts, unforeseen changing personalities, enlarged dimensions and spaces. All these elements are part and parcel of new public spaces. Without a beginning of E-education, citizens would not be able to understand their world and its inhabitants anymore. It is important to remember *how the* expression 'E-education' not only stands for 'electronic' but also for 'enhancement' as related to 'education'.

§ 4 The EU example

It fascinates to observe how in the European Union many of the above questions and experiences received widespread attention, often even more than in
the US. The European Union Commission (which is the central governing
institution of the Union) draws attention to the necessary implementation of
all types of electronic data provision since the 1980s. The mastering of computers and electronic instruments goes with educating in the practice and uses
of those media and related communication instruments, and with them the
realization of E-education and E-governance.

It's astonishing in this context how Estonia (one of the new Member States
and former Soviet Union Member State, only an EU Member state from May
1, 2004 on) has a higher degree of computerization in public space than any of
the other EU Member States. Internet access is omnipresent in public spaces.
Internet workstations and café's are signaled in the towns with public signs
that do not differ from ordinary traffic signs, and the familiar "@"—sign seems
a generally known and accepted mark. The argument is that one has to fight
computer illiteracy because that lack of knowledge and skills makes E-governance ineffective.

E-governance exemplifies what E-education strives to publicly and innova-
tively display. E-*information* is widely provided, so that active participation
and skilful articulation of opinion are made possible in all public spaces. The
tendency is to identify legal space and public space, where persons as a *citizen*
(public space) and as a *subject* endowed with inalienable rights (legal space)
form one identity. Would this identity not represent the unity of being
informed and being responsible? If this can be realized, then the idea of a

responsible citizen works, and E-*education* appears to be the great instrument for enhancing civic responsibility.

That observation focuses again the comparison between information and education. It seems that a transition from information to education (in which information is weighed, considered, and adapted) is basic to the engendering of a personal identity. The central question in public space that lays the groundwork for action, activity, and responsibility in public, is the *"who am I"* question. This question is, however, not unequivocal—it has many layers.

The "I" is a person, but also a subject of law, a citizen in a state, a member of a national community, an indispensable point of reference in a story or in detecting a center amidst the multiple layers of personality features. All those aspects are more important and complicated than just social roles to play. The original question, "who am I", is subject of education and therefore predominant in the many frames of electronically mastered and engendered reality. They show how information forms an important basis and that only the *integration* of all aspects and fragments is ultimately decisive. The latter is fruit of education, not of information alone.

There is another essential element within the overall picture. *Information* presupposes that data embedded in what will be named "the reality" is not a subject of further reflection or of critical proof. Presenting data is believed to be an act that contains an evidence qualified as "almost natural", an evidence suggesting that data can always be compared, falsified, or whatever one wishes to do to it. This presupposition is a basis in education, where a "test" almost naturally includes comparison, falsification, and the like. Consequently, there is no room for radical doubt in a Cartesian sense, no questioning of metaphysical dimensions, and not even a "to be or not to be" consideration.

In contrast, *education* inherently possesses reflective mechanisms, such as well-guided discussions about the truth of statements, debates among multiple opinions and interrogations pertaining to statements. These viewpoints and opinions are the result of education itself, the fruit of having learned to perceive life from multiple angles and having learned to judge accordingly.

This is encapsulated in one of the three major principles of E-education, the principle of *multiplicity*. To see reality as not evident by itself is the result of training and education. Philosophers would add that the joy of hesitating and of evaluating critically what comes to us as natural and evident results from a carefully educated technique of the human mind. This technique opens our eyes to the differences between "I" and "you", between a "self" and "others" and ultimately also for the fundamental plurality of reality features and formats when confronted with what we used to name "reality".

A *democratic deficit* is often quoted in this context, and could be understood as the flip side of multiplicity in life. That is not a shiny philosophical remark. The remark firmly underlines the importance of our earlier observation that there is a difference between the "informed citizen" and the "responsible citizen" and that *information* does not automatically lead to *action* unless education plays its mediation role. A clear example is how nations and other social conglomerates provide enormous quantities of information and allow enormous costs to be expended for information without any increase noticed in the democratic consciousness of the population. The question has been often formulated in the context of the recent global spreading of E-communication.

How come? Does it help to speak about a *democratic deficit*, like the EU commission did many times and on many occasions? There are many motives summed up in EU discussions about this deficit. They vary from a deficient functioning of the European Parliament to neglect stimulating EU citizens to develop any interest in non-national affairs. Such motives reach deeply into the constitution of the Union itself. An important example is where abstract centers of power and decision-making do not contact organizations and individuals properly, although they are responsible for life in conventional structures such as regions and patriotic provinces. Distance, lack of public understanding, deficient language, group feelings too strong to function in a structure of rule-following, subversion and perversion of decisions originating in unfamiliar languages and far away capitals, indeterminacy of the common good, or even straightforward xenophobia color the deficit problem. They will do so as long as information has not changed its character.

One motive has our particular attention. A democracy must be engendered in the mind of its *citizens*, who consider themselves as bearers of this precious ideal. The "who am I" question plays its central role again. But citizenship in the EU is not an unequivocal answer, it is rather a complex matter: (a) Citizens are born in a Nation-State and have their citizen rights by birth. That general rule knows its variations and differences among the Member States of the Union. (b) They acquire their EU citizenship on the basis of belonging to that national Member State. However, (c) large majorities of Europeans do not feel any deeply rooted commitment to their Nation-State and rather identify with the Region of their birth. This triple adherence is complex enough to cause psychological and legal conflicts.

These conflicts are nowadays intensified by the large numbers of migrants, who by definition do not have any of these ties but want the same rights because of their own history, their share in the national economy, their contribution to public life. So the deficit appears to be an identity crisis. Apart from all other items to discuss and that have been discussed, such as compliance with Union ideals or problems with the Union's inherent rule-following and positivist approaches to immense social and economic issues, there is one towering unsolved question. *In what public space are citizens supposed to play their role?*

The question is not irrelevant. The notion of the Union being the space within which citizens have to concretize a new legal order suffers indeed from conflict-loaded identity problems. Again there is the insight that "well informed citizens" are not automatically "active and responsible citizens." The theme "information and education" is clearly exemplified in this case.

Would the emerging *E·* culture achieve results? An electronically equipped public space could enhance human sovereignty, demystify technology, and put

E-technology in the hands of the actors in public space, thus becoming the starting point for a deliberative political community. However, that requires much more than the emphasis on the Internet, a one-sidedness that excludes the virtual or characterizes the virtual as unreal and unrealistic. What fits our discussion about information and education is *the question of whether E-enabled acting leads to changes in behaviors and consequently in society.*

Several conclusions can be offered in view of the relations between information and education in an *E·* culture.

The *first* is that information without the support of education is not meaningful at all.

Second, all information needs social and individual skills to manage and understand it. To develop those skills is the far-reaching and basically important task of E-education.

Third, the concept of education reaches far beyond the idea, so popular in the seventies and eighties in Europe, that life is a learning process with a life-long duration.

Fourth, and most important, one should recognize how the major emphasis in the expression "E-education" itself remains on "education" without neglecting and even with most powerfully integrating the technical as well as philosophical dimensions of the process of the "E-" in which communication is truly at stake.

PART II: EXPRESSIBILITY

§ 1 Introduction

The word "expressibility" is a neologism, introduced by philosophers such as John Searle, which fulfils a role in contemporary debates on speech act theory. Do we have the power to always express ourselves, to say clearly what we want to say, and are our speech acts sufficient to communicate everything that we want to bring into communication?

The core problem is not the clarity of expressions or our mastering of a language, not even the question whether we can be clear in one language and never in another. The problem is, *whether a linguistic utterance can be simultaneously characterized as an action*. The relation between an utterance and an action is essential for the concept of communication.

Included is a heavyweight philosophical problem. If we are able, by means of linguistic communication, to perform such a type of speech act, we unite in the act of communication both presentation and representation of reality in the form of action and utterance. If it appears that our language allows us to do so, then this would lead to a further conclusion. It would regard our ability to express, to articulate, eventually to name what the Ancient Greek philosophers understood to be a *Holon*—a totality beyond our expressions and communication. Is not such a totality, although a philosophical problem in its own right, the essence of education? And do we ever approach that totality by words? Does the E-language enable us to concretize such an approach and enhance the efficacy of our words? In other words: does the E-language, the "off-computer language" as well as the "computer language" in our communication with students, allow us *to better express the innermost* HOLISTIC *dimensions of education?*

§ 2 Holism

It is not our goal to present a definitive theory of holism in education, nor of holism in language. But holism is an important feature of any consideration of communication between subjects, the more so where non-human objects play a role that is equivalent to the roles of human subjects in communication This idea represents the revolutionary feature of e-communication today. A holistic approach in education shows the importance of non-human subjects, that is electronic machines and their contribution to enhancing the quality of human communication. To understand this, one needs first be informed about holism as a philosophical approach.

A major argument is that we all would like to think and understand the *whole*, but in striving to do so only seem to express the elements which constitute our knowledge and insight pertaining to that whole. This is frustrating in the case of education. Our speech and thoughts solely touch *elements* of the whole so that we are never able to speak about the *whole* itself, as it is! Our concepts and words, speech acts and arguments about the 'whole' are probably never reliable. That is complex and confusing in education, and underlines a situation of non-communication with reality. The consideration of this nature itself seems to be grounded in an apparent contradiction: he who wishes to perceive the whole, needs the analytical approach—with the effect that he does not reach his goal to perceive more than the results of his analytical mind.

This is just an example for the general structure at hand. Holism is the contrast of everything we think and of everything we try to reach with our methods of logic, philosophy or analysis. So, do we ever get out of our patterns of thought? These thought patterns and methods repeat the analytical approach, even in phenomenology—and in doing so; annihilate before our eyes what we want to perceive.

This seems a challenging issue pertaining to communication. Does our communication ever reach any approaching of the whole? Is Holism ever a genuine human experience? Or do we solely experience the 'whole' as the totality of all the elements we envision, but never the totality itself, which manifests itself in the embodiment of the student before our eyes? Looking at the student with these thoughts in mind, one is attempted to remember Wittgenstein. He said: "Not, however, as if to this end (seeing the student before us as a whole) we had to hunt out new facts; it is, rather, of the essence of our investigation that we do not seek to learn anything *new* by it. We want to understand something that is already in plain view. For *this* is what we seem in some sense not to understand. The problems are solved, not by giving new information, but by arranging what we have always known"[xxvii].

Three considerations about the relationships between our analytical attitude and the holistic property of communication are important.

First: Always perceiving the constitutive elements if one wishes to perceive the whole is a matter of method, i.e. of culture and culturally shaped thought patterns, and not a matter of ontological nature. It is, in other words, indicating how *we* proceed, and not how *nature* is. The common sense describes our cultural habits and deeply embedded frames of perception, and suggests "you cannot observe everything at the same time and as a whole". How would our electronic machines answer that observation? On the one hand, they are super-reductionist machines, because they are artifacts built upon binary parts and programming procedures. On the other, they are not blocked by the limits of our perception, which is a matter of neurology and brain structure.

Again, the computer shows us something to learn or at least to consider seriously in this context. 'Totality' seems an idea that functions at the background of our worldview. The idea furnishes the justification and ethical approval of nearly unlimited technological and scientific developments and advancements. This also is true of the social sciences, including studies in communication.

Second, there is an interesting variation of this theme. It is in the idea that our impossibility to perceive and to estimate the whole, even in another person, should be *an accepted risk* in social communications, for instance in education, and in science and technology. Is not the story of the great technological developments and the never ending stories of modern achievements, for instance in medicine and biology today, the story of *accepted risks*? And why should we then not accept them in education, especially when we introduce non-human subjects in educational relations, when they already appear to be an important issue in the entirety of our culture? There are examples enough to satisfy the critical mind, such as *accepted risks* in pharmacology, in medical practices, in psychiatric treatments, in biology as well as the global acceptance of human rights doctrine. They all belong to the profile of modern society. Changing those risks and accepting those transformations (if we can do that at all) would most probably endanger our social life.

The ontological basis of our everyday life is at stake. Technology in general suggests that things are being like they are. They suggest continuity in our ontological views of reality (a clearly determinable constancy in 'being'). But the debate about holism suggests the inverse, namely that 'there are' parts and wholes, and they are the 'furniture' of nature and our social life. How to solve this?

Third, we have to emphasize that the problem of parts and wholes does not necessarily sustain a mechanistic vision of reality. Smuts, who forwarded holism as an important philosophical perspective, suggests that all forms of being are striving towards a totality[xxviii]. Kant already mentioned how the human person is the most complete totality, and we acknowledge his insight especially in educational communications. Or, is the human person solely a totality in and with the State, as Hegel suggested? We acknowledge that insight where we perceive education as the creation of a complete form of personal citizenship. So one appreciates Kant as well as Hegel, and accepts both sides.

However, there is more to say. Modern biology, neurology or brain research suggests that human persons are moral or social entities, and as such need to be perceived as a whole. These sciences rather suggest that (biological) life itself should be seen as a whole, and humans as well as other animal species take part in this cosmos. One should notice that biology tends to become a modern epistemology, a new theory of knowledge.

It seems that a basis for this new epistemology is in the understanding that fragmentation reigns without exception. Even holism itself must to describe itself in terms of parts and fragments, although it can demonstrate itself wholly in the perception of another person, his look or touch, which creates the experience of wholeness beyond fragments. With what should a theoretical insight in communication engage itself—with experience of the otherness of the other as a whole, or with the analysis of the other as a composite of parts and fragments?

§ 3 Expressibility

Expressibility is about words and speech acts. Can we express what we think to mean, to intend, to load our speech acts with? The question is rather simplistic in view of the philosophical and social problems involved[xxix]. During the last decades of the twentieth century, at least three mainstreams of philosophical consideration came to the fore.

The *first* mainstream was proposed by thinkers who understood the major role of metaphysics in the debate about communication and the whole. They deplored what they called "the loss of metaphysical thinking" which always was the embedding of the *Holon* (Greek word for 'the whole'). A "new metaphysics" should transcend, for example, the traditional Kantian philosophy, pertaining to the person as a moral entity that, because of its moral character, was 'a whole'.

The *second* mainstream was of so-called "post-modern" authors, artists, and philosophers. They were convinced that one has to leave the "modern" behind since after modernity evolves a different culture with a reorientation of values and norms in society. The "modern" period was oppressive, left out the way our notions of being and totality were constructed and only a deconstruction activity could liberate our ideas and thoughts about *unity*, *wholeness* and *being*.

A *third* mainstream introduced "negative metaphysics" and attempted to develop Kantian metaphysics as a new basis for understanding language and communication, as Jürgen Habermas[xxx] formulated in the context of his theory of communication. This theoretical project leads to a confrontation with the reality of the student, his education included. The student represents the *Holon* in everyday life. His sheer existence does not allow any further abstract analysis. Is not every analysis based on fragments instead of the totality of a life? And is not every encounter with a living person a repetition of the problems to understand the *Holon* in our thoughts, and in social reality as well?

One could conclude that Habermas' theory of communication also encounters the problem of the inexpressible *Holon*. His theory, although critically recapitulating postmodernism, is yet founded on relations between a sender and a receiver, between an *ego* and an *alter* as if these were naturally given facts. Also his ideas carry the burden to explain how this basic assumption can lead to the reality of the Other, who—in the words of Kant—lives by the grace of being acknowledged and recognized as a person by the other participants in social context. A confrontation with the *Holon*, which is manifest in the student in education, seems to be a stumble stone in any communication theory that sustains education. This view is problematic as long as the ego-alter scheme grounds a view on communication in education.

Our preceding chapter explained how the *dialogue* might show an alternative in this context and leads to a different articulation of the *Holon*. We rephrase this insight in practical terms. A student is continuously involved in dialogues (of all kinds) and lives in the context of a great variety of narratives. In that light, one could conclude, a Word itself, realized by an appropriate speech act, is the *Holon* par excellence!

A Word, as well as the Good, is related to the question of expressibility. Words as well as our expressions of the good, the just, the beautiful, the valuable and a life in dignity (all those words pertain to students in education) seem to depend on an inadequate language, a speech that goes for analogy and analysis, but lacks the power of immediacy to grasp meanings in their totality. What electronics can contribute in this regard, especially in view of the feeling of inadequacy pertaining to our spoken language, is a field of research in the decades to come.

E-education is indeed a fresh start, but keep four aspects in mind:

(a) The Whole, even in the figure of a human person, is not a simple datum of culture or of concepts of the human mind alone.

(b) The expression "the One IS" cannot be excluded from, nor entirely expressed through language and communication. The meaning of that expression changes with the dimensions of culture, place and history.

(c) Expressiveness pertaining to the Whole seems to lead to an universalistic attitude. Habermas, for instance, seems to suggest that each human speech act is not only determined by fragmented but also by unifying meanings.

(d) Habermas' theory became famous because of the idea that we all have this unified meaning in our mind when we speak, and that all of us perform our speech acts in what he calls an "ideal speech situation".

There is no way to deny that those remarks imply a political philosophy colored by democratic ideals. They renew the old idea of a society based on the perfection of a social contract—a soft individualism, one could say. A formula, which Habermas often applies, shows this perspective. Our speech activity and our care for a healthy expressiveness are based on the fact that we strive for *"an undamaged intersubjectivity as a projection of future symmetric relations of free and mutual recognition"*, he proclaims. All elements of our considerations in the preceding paragraphs can be found in that one sentence!

One should reconsider what has been formulated about the innateness of our expressiveness. The core problem is not in the clarity of expressions in a language. The problem is even not whether we can be clear in one language and never in another. The problem we have to face is whether *a linguistic utterance can be simultaneously characterized as an action.* That relationship between utterance and action in view of reality is essential for understanding communication.

John Searle wrote in this context[xxxi]: "I take it to be an analytic truth about language that whatever can be meant can be said. A given language may not have a syntax or a vocabulary rich enough for me to say what I mean in that language but there are no barriers in principle to supplementing the impoverished language or saying what I mean in a richer one"

An implicit reference to a totality of language and speech is at the center of this sentence. However, one must critically state that the PERFORMANCE *of a meaningful speech act differs from the* MEANING *of a specific sentence in a specific language.* As far as a linguistic performance is concerned, one asks whether a speech act is a constitutive unit of language and speech—or do there exist languages *without* speech acts, which are nevertheless meaningful? That consideration provokes another question. How are connections between speech acts constituted so that they form the blueprint for social action and communication?

Many elements are involved here. We distinguish the speech act itself and what the speaker means, furthermore what the uttered sentence means, what the speaker intends, what hearers are supposed to understand, and what common rules make understanding and communication possible. A whole set of presuppositions is at work in any speech-related situation.

One should keep in mind, however, what Smuts, the greatest advocate of holism, suggested: "...how could the part envisage the whole? The question remains of central interest in all educational settings, and is of immediate relevance for introducing the E• factor, the enhancement of education by means of electronics in the realm of communication.

PART III: WORDS

§ 1 Introduction

We stated in the preceding chapters that words and meanings are essential for each type of communication, and that one needs social and individual skills in order to manage and understand information. Language is the milieu of education, it was said, and that is of even greater importance when natural languages and the language of electronics come together and reinforce each other. And one of the most favorable settings for reading and conversation is an educational institution, E-education centers included. Finally one experienced how words are algorithms, containing complex meanings and keys to access reality. A strong and most vital correlation between *word* and *world* was emphasized.

That is extremely relevant in communication and essential to education as the max of communicative situations. On the one hand is the importance of meaning and word being closely tied together, almost forged into a one specific entity. On the other hand, however, there is the pedagogic experience of how managing words goes with an enhancement of understanding words!

These issues lead to elaborate theoretical, and even philosophical, investigations, some of which have been discussed in previous chapters and the first pages of this chapter. Do not forget how words used in various sets of communication also require different approaches!

A REMARK ON THE COMPOSITION OF THIS TEXT HAS THEREFORE TO FOLLOW:
The next pages will be dedicated to the task of provoking variations in set and approach, with the use of different words as a consequence. We give a number of examples of words and expressions that are most commonly used by teachers in the classroom, in an 'off-computer' context as well as in combination with computer guided conversations—sometimes even as a verbal interruption of computer generated language. And we add some issues of the language and the conversational structures that teenagers use among themselves.

It is philosophically and theoretically important to notice that such explanation of words and their meaning also turn our attention away from analytical language and expressiveness towards dialogic uses and interpretations of the same vocabulary and exchange of words.

§ 2 Situations

A. Teacher-Student Conversations

The use of words and their different meanings in the frame of various situations, with analytic as well as dialogic approaches, leads us to distinguish five different educational appearances. Let us first approach some key notions of the *teacher-student conversations*.

Our comments are on *self-centered* language, furthermore the *dialogic* language that creates *peace*, then the languages of *judgments* and of *tests* and finally the language of *encouragement*.

The Self Centered and the Dialogic Teacher

1. Self Centered Sentences

A common expression from the large range of daily expressions in educational communication is the question *"Do you understand what I am telling you?"* The sentence is spoken daily, and sounds almost natural to teachers and students. Sometimes it's an outcry, but often it's an automatically pronounced attempt to create togetherness, watchfulness, or attention and it's sometimes the expression of a last resort in a difficult situation. Do you understand?

There are several ways to answer the question "Do you understand?"

Students.

• "Do you understand?" and the answer of the student is "no"! What to do? It's either the end of the learning process, or the teacher must find a way to start that process all over again. In the meantime, nothing is learned, no educational goals are reached, and there is silence all over the room, no matter whether the student was honest and did not understand, or he was simple uttering a one-syllable protest against the learning situation and the teacher.

• The student can have thought: "do you, teacher, doubt my ability to understand?" So his answer "no" has nothing to do with the teaching materials and his learning abilities—he is insulted and the negation expresses that emotional situation. What to do?

• A further differentiation of the insulted feeling is that the teacher's question awakened a *moral* disillusion: "does the teacher mean to say that I am a bad student?" How bad am I, and how good is he—is that not implied in his expression?

• Sometimes, there is no audible answer at all to this question "Do you understand?" The student suddenly feels that he is not able to judge whether he is familiar with the issue, and becomes confused: "how do I know whether I really understood?" The silence is deafening, and very important to listen to.

• There is still another variation on that theme, namely that the student replies immediately to the question "Do you understand?" with a "Yes". There might be two effects: (1) the student knows his answer will not immediately be checked, and thus creates an undetermined status among his classmates, and (2) he causes his classmates to think: "why am I so stupid not to understand, whereas he did and I did not!"

Teachers.

• So much for the students, with some of the most obvious consequences and implications. There is only one important semantic consequence for the teacher, when raising the question: "Do you understand what I am telling you?" He provokes a termination of his teaching responsibility by implicitly saying "it's not my role or task to make all this clear to you, it's your role to understand, and you are responsible for that!" All the above-mentioned student answers are in fact a reaction to that semantic implication. So what has the teacher to consider, if his goal is the creation of a good communication with the students?

2. Dialogic Sentences

The question "Do you understand what I am telling you?" is easily changed into its opposite. Whereas the "I" of the teacher is predominant in this sentence, and blocks all possibilities of the students to really participate in a common problem, namely to understand an issue, the sentence "Do I make myself clear?" opens up that activity to full participation. One could say that the positioning of the teacher's "I" itself changes the communication from inaccessibility to accessibility and shared interests in the interplay. In view of the general outline of any theory of communication, the conclusion is that only the *positioning* (not even the exchange) of one word makes the difference. Why?

The answer is simple: in the first sentence, the *You* is made responsible, and in the second the *I*. The communication structure between teacher and student is not, that the student is initially responsible for his understanding of an issue determined on beforehand by the teacher! The teacher teaches, and there is a shared responsibility between teacher and student, not an exclusive responsibility of the student.

• Although the "I" is also central in the reformulated question "Did I make myself clear?"—the question is by no means a self-centered question. The wording shows that the teacher understands it is his or her responsibility to make things clear, and the student has to answer about the teacher's activity, not about his own success or failure. That is in essence the structure of a dialogic attitude.

• If the student answers "no", then the effect of that negation is totally different from the situation described before. The issue remains open to be clarified. No moral luggage to carry and no feelings of failure, because the process of clarification is on its way and all other students are equally involved.

• It remains perfectly possible that the student answers the question "Did I make myself clear?" with an "I do not know" or a simple "no". But they feel engaged in the process of clarification, and are therefore not able to abruptly end the process or to express the negative feeling "leave me alone". They might be driven by the dialogic structure of the conversation, and discover that the conversation is not on the issue at hand but on the clarification itself, in which they take part! So they should be guided to answer "Let me find out!" or "Let me think about it!" Habermas' "ideal speech situation" was mentioned before, and his suggestion, that we all have a unified and common meaning in our mind when we speak, will be practiced in that newly appropriated expressiveness. Was not our leading motive in the question when *a linguistic utterance can be simultaneously an action*? Here it is the case!

• One should not leave out a strong emotional component in the classroom. The word "clear" is emotionally different from the words "understanding" and "telling you". It creates a friendly atmosphere and an environment in which the student feels invited to participate. The dialogic attitude does not cause an inner conflict in the student, nor a competitive feeling about his position with his classmates. To teach is to be on the way—and students must internalize that adage!

The Power of Dialogue

The power of a dialogic attitude is important and reaches into all parts of the communication. Some final examples should be considered.

• The questions "why?" and "what for?" are not incidental or only important in specific situations, for instance where the dialogue gets stuck or the problems at hand require a further consideration. On the contrary: those little words should constantly accompany the communication. To know the reason for and the direction chosen in communication is not the privilege of the teacher! Students and teachers should be informed and be able to reconsider all the time. "Why" is not a childish question, but ties teacher and student together.

The same counts for "what for". In short: if there is not a common denominator embraced by both, by students as well as teachers, then the education communications are already endangered. Teachers who claim the privilege of determining the "what for" and mastering the "why" are self-centered and do not display any fragment of a dialogic attitude.

• This is also the case in the teachers' formulations. The conception of a question and its answer is vital in any education situation. Most of the time, teachers display a non-dialogic attitude in providing their students with answers, sometimes even before the students are able to raise a question. It is more stimulating and shows more respect for the student, if answers are not given at all, and the major teaching activity is the weighing of a diversity of questions. But those questions should be really questions, and not just a duplicate of the answers that the teacher wants to hear!

• Further, there are moral dimensions involved in the teacher-student contact.

One aspect of that difficult segment of communication is in the pretension of *equal rights*. The equality of the rights position is an issue between students and teachers only in a critical situation, when the communication is on the verge of breaking down. There are never single, isolated rights. A right is not a single thing possessed by one specific individual. No right alone can ever decide a conflict. All those ideas on rights are a form of self-centeredness. And it is left out that rights are one side of a coin and obligations are the other side. The equality of rights pertains to the balance of rights and obligations, outweighing both in balance of a self and others.

Second is the use of morally loaded expressions. "That's a silly question!" means not a depreciation of the person that originated the utterance. It means often, that the teacher does not want to consider the question and does not spend the time to find an answer or any other form of compensation. The qualification "silly" is morally defective and should be avoided in any education communication.

Judgments and Tests

All teaching activities and all other sorts of educational communications are loaded with judgments and tests, where the teachers seem to take an opposite position to the student. Is that compatible with the dialogic attitude as described here? Or do judgments and tests show that the dialogue is ultimately unrealistic? Dialogues might perhaps be good for some of the phases in the contact between teacher and student, but not realistic for the entire educational relationship. This consideration shows an institutional aspect that we do not discuss here. It would lead to a sociological study of education systems, which is not what we're about here. But one could indeed focus on key words that relate to judging students and to performing tests.

1. Judgments

• *Focus*. One of the most frequently used expressions is linked with the focus of a student. "He cannot focus" says the teacher. What does this mean? The major disadvantage of the expression is that everybody seems to understand, but nobody can formulate or define its precise content. The student is not at all involved in this judgment, and the teacher is not able to clarify either to the student or to parents and other educators what he precisely means. If questioned, the teacher answers most of the times: "I am talking to him and he is in a different world"—which means that the student can focus very well, but prefers to focus on other matters than those brought to his attention by the teacher. Ultimately the judgment "he cannot focus" does not pertain to the student but rather to the teacher, who in essence declares: "I do not succeed in attracting his attention". That changes the emphasis from the student to the teacher—which is for the teacher often a disagreeable turn in the communication. It's not the student that does not perform, but the teacher. The teacher apparently has to change his speech strategies, and then the student will focus!

As a consequence, the focus is not the product of the student. The student's focus depends upon the teacher's ability to create an atmosphere of togetherness and a general climate of involvement. One encounters again the difference between self centered and dialogic attitudes in teaching. The judgmental observation "he cannot focus" places the "I" of the teacher central, whereas a student's focus blossoms when a "we" is created and put in a central position, socially as well as in the language pattern. The judgment shows the student's need for recognition, acknowledgement, and socialization.

• *Bad.* Teachers complain about *bad students*. They start their classroom sessions, and say in a loud voice: "Quiet please!" but there is no silence in the room. It is, he says, because that's a class with bad students. They don't listen, and do not interrupt their conversations and activities when he demands it. But what did he or she do? There was a noisy environment, and he added to it by shouting: "Quiet please". His words were of the same noise level as all others. His utterances did not distinct themselves from all others and were therefore of no interest to any of the students.   Instead, if you want your students to be attentive and to listen to you, speak in a lower voice. They don't hear you in that case? Perhaps, but they see that you are speaking, and they may start to be interested in what you have to say, and encourage others not to disturb their own interest in your speech. It is contradictory to *shout* the word "Quiet" because the meaning of the word contradicts the reality of the communication. And, what is more, a quiet environment is a safe and friendly environment, which invites full participation. The students experience how they are free from tension and anxiety—which is a precondition for successful teaching and learning. A bad class? Who is making that claim?

After three times shouting "Quiet please!" without audible success, a teacher may want to say: "I don't know what to do, the students are so bad!" What did he say? This phrase is like the others: if you listen carefully, you find out that the students aren't being described here, the teacher is. If a cheeky and impudent student would have listened to that utterance, and said: "OK, find yourself another job!" he would really have been right, although perhaps impolite. If the student is bad, then the teacher has to find out, create alternatives on which the judgment is based, find other means to finally judge positively. It must be emphasized that E-education has many advantages in this regard. The teacher's skills and fantasy, as well as the wealth of computer programs and the fascination of the machines play a role in the improvement of the student's situation. To claim that there are bad students is a complaint about one's own dispositions.

• The same is true when judgmental expressions are used, such as "the child has a low self-esteem", or "the child is behind" or "disabled" or "not at level". These are judgments to express that the teacher's requirements are not being met. Perhaps the requirements are not issued by the teacher himself or herself, and may have an institutional meaning. But even in that case, the teacher functions as a translator, and the expressions show that his translator-activity has failed one way or another. If a child is behind a mean standard of his classmates, what then has the teacher done to help the student? Is that standard really fit for the teacher-student relationship at this moment, and could other persons offer help or other instruments change the situation? "Esteem", "behind", "disabled", "at level" are judgmental expressions, which confront the teacher with his own abilities to meet the criteria of the institutions.

2. Tests

What do tests measure? That is a general question, and not exclusively relevant in education communications. Tests are omnipresent in our society, from medical sciences and the pharmaceutical industries to market analyses, from job satisfaction to partner matching, from political debates to philosophical considerations. We always take a test, especially in communicative contexts, not only in schools, universities, or businesses, but also—and by no means always metaphorically—in social relationships.

So, what is at stake? To test seems to be a deeply rooted habit in Western culture. From our earliest years on we are affected by how we did on the test. They helped to determine what schools we attended, how we met friends or even a partner. What did the tests measure? We did and do not know; the tests often seem a strange ritual without which we are not a reliable and serious person in social life. Moreover, a student does not do only what in one specific test is measured, but he also performs very well in one test and absolutely catastrophically in another—even if the tests are closely related. Further, intelligence tests particularly show differences in people that are close to each other in life, perform the same tasks, and have the same life style and habits.

• "He failed the test!" What does this say? Did he fail what was *in* the test, or did he fail in relation to issues that are *outside* the test? Is he behind because he failed the test? One often hears this. Is this truly the case? Apparently not, if one looks at his behavior and general learning profile. So, who failed: *the student*, who lives every moment anew and changes all the time, from growing cells to exploring all sorts of behaviors—or *the school*, who had to prepare him for the test as a test of changing instead of fixated issues at hand? What language is used here: *to fail* is also a *downward* movement, a deception, a disillusion.

The word "test" itself has a predominantly situational meaning. But a test does not take changing situations into account. Tests have long lives, longer than any tested person is in the situation to be tested! How can we leave this context of authoritarian and oppressive meanings behind, and come to dialogical meanings? Change the word, and create another content. Go for *"evaluation"* instead of *"test"*. An evaluation is dynamic, stretches over time, and emphasizes the good and valuable things in a person's life. Insufficiencies are put in perspective. They are also changing with the rest of the student fragments of life!

3. Encouragement

There is no one definitive conclusion to be drawn from these observations. But they might help to broaden our awareness of the fact that words are like an environment: words shape, color, determine meanings, and enhance possibilities in the mind and communicative activity of the speaker. Speakers create their own listeners! That is surely a basis for education in and outside the classroom.

The general tendency of those observations is to highlight the fact that a self-centered language creates meanings that are clearly negative for the student, who is involved in all layers of meanings implied in the words of the teacher. Dialogic language, on the contrary, creates freedom, and inspires and challenges the best in a student. That language causes equality beyond a balance of individual rights, it causes cooperation beyond obligation, and it creates an atmosphere of peace and quiet that is so much needed in all educational settings—look through the windows of our classrooms!

B. Student-Student Conversations

How do we discover the specific features of student-to-student conversations and their social patterns? We concentrate in this section and in the next chapter on *Peer Groups* to elucidate the dynamics of linguistically relevant behaviors. It is clear that the dynamics of students having conversations with other students differ from the dynamics of student-teacher communications.

Peer groups contain individuals of the same age and/or social status who share identical values and interests. The groups create a strong feeling of *belonging*, which is a most important issue for teens today. Forms of belonging to peer groups, sub-cultures, and friendships change frequently, but all have a strong socializing effect. Peer life for teens is, not unlike the Web and electronic games, predominantly adult-free. Yet, at another social level, adult norms and values also determine peer-life. Teen authority emerges in peers rather often in parallel to the parental relations at home. Peers are almost without exception same-gender groups, but there are father/mother/child/figures in these groups, and these produce family-like relationships and communication patterns.

Peer groups show how adolescents have *belonging* (as formatted in institutional life) in common. There are interactive and e-educational situations, in which awareness of this common ground is enhanced and skills to behave more efficiently and responsibly in key institutions of modern life are acquired. Responsive citizenship results from an enhanced awareness of socialization. Teens and adults experience the major denominations of social life in the wider context of the institutions for which they become educated.

Electronically enhanced education (E-education) focuses in particular the enhancement of responsive citizenship; it also helps adolescents to understand and to manage worries—not through psychotherapy or authoritarian guidance but by means of interactive exploration of the major semantic dimensions of worries. It was explained in previous chapters how deeply this interactivity relates to electronic means in education. Parallel with this observation is the insight that primarily words with their implied meanings (indeed: either self-centered or dialogically oriented) constitute a most stimulating and enhancing environment in their own right.

Several fundamental issues are important here:

• Adolescents are quite often "contemplators" in relation to their own partici-pation in peer life. They think about future changes in their life in terms of the peer mentality, more generally in terms of friendship and mutual recognition, and need repeatedly a further consideration of their motivations and future behaviors.

• Adolescents experience their choice of friends and the construction of peer groups as an exclusively *private* performance. They need to actively consider the social implications of their peer life as dominated by norms and values of specific institutions (such as schools) or life styles and civic life of the family.

• Adolescents have in this regard difficulties accepting and understanding how peer participation is based on more or less fixed value judgments, in contrast to their temporary state of affairs. The development of skills to explore such insights leads to new forms of self-understanding and accomplishes identity formation. These skills form the basis of responsive citizenship and enhance the quality of adolescent life.

• If communication training can reinforce such skills, than this training should be used at home, in school curriculums, and as after school programs, in train-ing situations in our social institutions, community centers, civic centers and administrations. An age-directed coaching is required in all those cases. Indications pertaining to 'teachers training' lay the groundwork for an impor-tant advisory service that complements this type of training, in which indeed "words form an environment":

1
"Only One More..."

"Let us accept Charles as a member of our groups. It's only one more..." is an argument and a sentence that is often listened to. But: is it correct and what is its innermost meaning? One could even be afraid that this sentence is again one of the expressions we characterized as 'self-centered'. So, let us imagine a game for the purpose of understanding and clarification.

E-education established a game on the creation of awareness about the often used argument that one additional person in an existing group, or one item in possession of a group used by an outsider, is just *"only one more"*, and is therefore beyond reasonable discussion. How can one object to the simple acceptance of another person, another item and another relationship? The game's purpose is to experience how *the mechanism of inclusion and exclusion,* for instance allowing a person to join or not allowing the use of an item, is *based on a complex arithmetic of relations.*

Students must understand how that arithmetic reaches far beyond individual decisions or value judgments. Allowing expansion of an existing group, the use of its possessions, or the merger with another group is an important decision because of the many and complex consequences involved.

It is clear to each educator that this exercise is of great importance to students in all life situations and in particular in the context of their peer situation. One should understand that *emotional arguments* and *value judgments* are not the only ones that determine decisions on size and scale of peer groups or on the use of group property by outsiders. Students should be aware of the limits of those emotional and value arguments. They can only use them after developing skills to make decisions on grounds of numerical and arithmetic nature, to put purely emotional reasoning into perspective, and to master the scale of their friendship activities. Let us imagine a closer look:

1. The first section of the game offers insight in the *numerical complexity of addition.* There is a group of four friends. That group remains numerically stable. Why? Is the argument: "…there will be only one more…" correct? No, the question is a false use of numbers, because it fails to address the increase in the number of relations within the group. . How many relations exist in a group of four? In a group of five? Of ten? What general arithmetic formula must be used to quickly answer that type of arguments and questions?

2. The next step is on the *addition of temporary group members*. The peer group of boys comprises four members. There is one member whose sister participates now and then, sometimes together with another friend. If the group is with the two girls, what numerical pattern of relations exists at that moment? One must observe and outline the increased complexity of decision-making in that latter case, and compare it to the pattern of the core group of four members.

3. There now follows *the inclusion of items* possessed by group members. The peer group has two members, Steve and Nick, who each own a car. How does the decision about the use of the car become more complex if the peer group members do not take into account that possession? In other words, do they agree to decide on the use of the cars as if they all were the proprietors of one of the two cars on an equal basis? What happens of the two girls become implied in this agreement? What happens to the notion of "personal/private property", which is a fundamental value notion in our society?

4. The consequences of inclusion and exclusion of members in a group are often misjudged. Take the following situation. A peer group of four boys considers merging with another peer group in their school class, which is "only a small group" of three. This sounds very reasonable. Formulate a judgment on what is really going to happen in the patterns of social relations of those peer groups, and consider the following agreements:

(a) The *two* groups of boys simply merge into *one* group. What to say about the *total* package of relationships?

(b) The two groups simply merge, but one of their members, who functions as the leader, tells the others that he wants 50% more weight in each decision of the new group than all others?

(c) The *two* groups merge only under the condition that the *two* girls—Dave's sister Rachel and her friend Maria—can participate

    (*) On an equal basis any moment they wish,

    (**) On an equal basis only after consensus in the boys' group,

    (***) On an equal basis only after a positive decision of the group leader.

(****) On an equal basis only including the use of the two cars by each of the girls.

At the end of these games (which can be completed by other games), the students should be able to withdraw from emotional, moral, and other judgments on face value, and include the arithmetical dimensions in their reasoning. The choices, preferences, etc. of the students confronted with these various situations form a sound basis for evaluation. "Only one more…" is an expression that seems more meaningful and more complex than our students are aware of in their daily conversations. The expression has also great importance for their future life in social institutions. These experiences might belong to the most important issues of their lives.

2

"So Many Pressures…"

It is generally known that peer group members complain about moral, behavioral, and other pressures. They are manifestly exerted by society through social institutions such as schools, families, churches, or political organizations. The complaint pertaining to "pressures" cannot be neglected in e-educational settings.

An additional E-education game introduces the problem so that the students acquire the skills *to recognize* and, in addition to this recognition, *to master* the pressure on them. Peer groups are to US adolescents the preferred tools to keep up with those pressures. This game's purpose is to enhance the students' awareness about such pressures, about their evaluation and their importance in peer life.

The game is constructed along two different lines: *first*, there is an *orientation* of the values that form general pressures on adolescent behavior. *Second*, there is a *weighing* of those pressures, in particular in as far as those pressures originate in adult requirements that are openly communicated.

1. *Investigating value orientations and pressures on peer groups.*

The program of the game first mentions a series of values and norms that cause pressures on adolescent behavior. Some arbitrarily chosen ones are:

smoking,

dieting,

drugs,

violence,

harassment,

sex,

sexual proclivity

environmental issues,

individualism,

human rights,

social duties.

This game/exercise now requires the following operations:

(a) Arrange the above values and norms into an order that is relevant to your behavior and preferences in a scale from 1–10

(b) Add to your order other values and norms that are important to you, and reconstruct the entire scale

(c) Arrange the order of values and norms as you think your various peer group members would do

(d) Make profiles from these orders and compare those profiles. What about your own profile, does it conform the group's profiles or does it disagree with them in any regard?

(e) Your expectations might comprise your future behavior. Many adolescents expect a change in their appreciation when growing older. Can you predict a profile for yourself in one year's time? In two years?

(f) What about your peer friends? Are there specific expectations for your and your peer friends' future, for instance with regard to your attitude towards the other gender, profession, possession, and property?

(g) Many of the normative pressures are caused not by individuals, but by institutions. Can you make a list of the most important institutions related to your social behavior? Consider such institutions as family, school, important groups, churches, civic centers, and others. Make a profile of their importance for yourself in as far as your behavior is concerned.

2. *Weighing pressures.*

Most of those pressures originate from adult life. The second issue of this game is on the weight those requirements acquire in adolescent life-situations. The game requires the following operation:

• Take the 10 points list of Game 1 and illustrate their weight:

(a) **As being *different* from each other**. Is the weight you give to issues of sex higher or lower than issues of violence? Of family matters higher than of peer groups? Of smoking habits higher than environmental behavior? Etc.

(b) **As being *relevant* when ordered in groups**: are sex and violence heavier weighted than your environment? Or (to combine all this in a different manner) do for instance drugs and smoking habits possess a heavier weight than human rights, or not?

(c) **From here, *"why-questions"* can be made operational**. If human rights, for instance, form a less heavy moral and behavioral pressure than sex, then why is this so, and what is the importance of the individual cause in the entire pattern?

(d) Human rights or environmental issues are less related to *you as an individual*. Is that a motive in your weighing the issues of that scale? Express the relevance of these items for your individual interest in quantitative judgments; put them on a scale in order to express your preferences as clearly as possible. Can you guess how your peer friends would profile themselves in that same context?

The games create many sheets and different pages, which are commented in group—and in private sessions. It should make peer group lives aware of their pressures, and promote discussions that otherwise would not take place.

3
"Are We Two Teams?"
—Peer Life versus Family Life—

Peers confront "peer life" and "family life" many times. This is mainly because the two share many characteristics and social functions. Families have *formal* social functions as good as peers do. Peers influence the emerging social *identity* of adolescents as families do. Peers and families both refer to related social *institutions*, such as schools, churches, etc.

The purpose of this E-education game is to have the students acquire a determinate insight into the common features of their own peer groups and their family. Emphasis is on the institutional features of family and peer group, and on how they relate to church, school, community, and other institutions.

Three major themes

are included in the construction of this game/exercise:

(1) Awareness of the student's *position* in family and peer group,

(2) Investigation of all *common* features and interests in both teams, and the *differences* among the common items, delete of that commonness included, and

(3) Understanding of the various types and styles of *interaction*

Individual boys might want to emphasize how the interest of the family team is *the continuation of the family*. The major interest of the peer group is to sustain positions in school and other social institutions, as well as to help them define an identity that is acceptable to their social environment and to themselves as individuals. A clear articulation of such findings can assist the student to fully profit from the game.

Styles of interaction are a further issue. It goes without saying that styles of interaction vary with the types of interaction in family and peer groups. The "hide and seek" play in family situations differs from those in peer groups. Authority is never absent, but digested differently. Hierarchical relationships exist continuously, but they emerge differently and are appreciated in a different manner. Peer groups suggest that authority and hierarchy are freely chosen, whereas they constitute obligations in family life.

This game starts with the establishment of a list of expressions, keywords, and core themes of their groups in peer—and family life. That list can guide the students expressive associations or thematic insight when they have to participate in the two teams that represent either peer groups or family groups.

4.
"The Principal's Desk"
—Composing a School Class Compared to a Peer Group—

There is an old saying that you do not choose your relatives, but you do choose your friends. The first seems a matter of fate whereas the latter seems the result of free and rational decision-making. Hence the peer remark "Classes are like family—they are not chosen, at least not by the students!" There are two parts in this E-education game.

The *first* part introduces to the mentioned saying. It should do so by representing a Principal of a large Middle School who, together with teachers and administrators, has the final responsibility to determine the composition of a school class. What are his materials, what is his major purpose, and what does he want to achieve, and what to avoid? Show the limits of his decision-making process in a role-play, and create a situation of clear alternatives from which to choose. Elucidate the final results and give a profile of the expectations of the Principal and his team. Finally, the student should be challenged to articulate his or her appreciation, after the experience of the student's interaction in this game.

The *second* part of this role-taking game focuses the student's feelings of freedom and rational decision-making. How is a peer group composed, how did the group come into life, how did others enter the group, and what are the purposes and/or limits to this group? Show the processes and phases of a peer group coming into life, and have the students make the comparison with family life. Create the opportunity to answer the question of how they define a peer group.

The Parts 1 and 2 of this section on "Situations" are decidedly different. The reasons for that difference are clear. Conversations between teachers and students show a clear emphasis on the meanings of words and expressions, whereas the situations in which these expressions are used remains relatively stable. However, conversations between students and students show an emphasis on contexts. Meanings of words and expressions vary with these contexts and depend upon the intensity of these expressive fragments. The first are objects of experiences that focus on the semantics, whereas the second depend largely on the social contexts. It might be clear that both clarify the complexity of meaning in communication beyond an analytical approach of the implied semantics. The virtues of a dialogic approach are demonstrated by imaginary games. Reading those drafts of games might already be instructive in this regard. The next chapter completes this consideration of the essence of communication (e-techniques included) by means of imagined dialogues in—and about peer groups.

CHAPTER IV

PEER GROUPS

§ 1 CHARACTERS

"PEER GROUPS" IS A SCRIPT FOR E-EDUCATION CENTERS WITH THE FOLLOWING CHARACTERS:

Nick, 16 years of age, 11th grade High School

Ritchie, 15 years of age, 10th grade High School

Dave, 15 years of age, 10th grade High School

Steve, 16 years of age, 11th grade High School

Rachel, sister of Dave, 13 years of age, 8th grade Middle School

Maria, friend of Rachel, 13 years of age, 8th grade Middle School

Michael, father of Dave, lawyer, 38 years of age

Esther, mother of Dave, 36 years of age

Mario, teacher, 28 years of age

Ben, teacher, 29 years of age

§2 PEER GROUPS

Part I: "PEERS ARE EVERYWHERE"

Scene 1: Pressures

Images and Sounds

Next to the crossing of a small and a major road is a little square, partially grass and partially concrete. An old bar, vending machines beer and sodas outside. There are two cars, an old Ford and an even older Nissan, four boys, drinking beer and sodas, some sitting on the hood of their cars. One is Dave, 15 years, 10th grade High School, the others are Steve, 16 years, 10th grade High School, owner of the Ford, Ritchie, 15 years, 10th grade High School, and Nick, 16 years, 11th grade High School, owner of the Nissan. A portable radio is put on the hood of the Nissan. Music plays challengingly loud.

Nick

I had to fight.

Ritchie

For what?

Dave

For that car?

Nick

To become one of us.

Dave

Where, when? I don't remember. Was I there?

Nick

Corner of Lincoln. Couple of months ago. Didn't know it was part of a ritual. Thought it was very serious, felt challenged.

Dave

So what?

Nick

I kicked as hard as I could. I didn't get hurt or complain.

Dave

They call that violence.

Nick

Why? We're not cops!

Steve

Any difference between them and us? Look at my Ford—they have the same!

Dave

Weapons, I guess.

Steve

You don't have a gun?

Dave

No, my Dad, he keeps it away.

Steve

Locked?

Dave

Don't know, I'm not interested.

Ritchie

Why did you fight that hard?

Nick

To be one of us.

Ritchie

Satisfied now?

Nick

Sure, what else? Look at us—the cars, the beers, sodas, girls watching, and waiting, being there. You're someone, no longer a nobody. Without taking risks you're nobody.

Steve

Yeah, a 'somebody.' Identity they call it. You knew?

Dave

Yeah. My Dad speaks that language.

Steve

To you?

Dave

No, what do you think? Speaks into his cell phone. He has a language for that. Succeeds to impress. Impresses to succeed!

Ritchie

Would you do it again?

Nick

What?

Ritchie

Fight for identity.

Nick

Of course. Like my Nissan. In fact, you always have to.

Dave

Think everybody has to. All the time. No?

Nick

But now, each of us managed.

Ritchie

For how long?

Nick

Doesn't matter. Now.

Dave

What do we do with it?

Steve

Don't know. Feel protected, have an address. Know what to do. Be backed up, when necessary. I'd back up all of you now. Don't know whether I can really trust anyone, but I guess I can some of you, yeah.

Nick

What? For doing what?

Dave

What to do…don't laugh. Everybody tells me what to do. Dad, schoolteachers, girls, church ministers, Mom, street corner workers, sisters, scouts, newspapers, book authors, janitors, physicians, bus drivers, police officers, you name it. A whole bunch of telling-what-to-do people. I hate that. Pressures.

Steve

Yeah. Even my pants tell me what to do, how to wear them, how to walk, how to look around…how to be *in* them!

Dave

I like them, by the way.

Steve

Great. What does it mean that you like them? You want them also? I don't care; I have them, here and now. They fit. You try to get them.

Dave

You do. Shut up.

Steve

Only after another drink. Soft. Had enough beer. Super. Shapes me…Talk about me after I'm gone, not to my face.

Dave

I don't.

Steve

You do. Everybody does.

Nick

What pressures? Don't you understand they want us to behave?

Dave

Behave? They constantly tell you what to do. Safe sex. Think before you go for it, protect yourself, don't risk passion; just go for your condom. Don't smoke, you'll die from cancer, lack of oxygen…don't drive that bumpy car, it spoils the environment with its fumes. Look at LA, Mexico City, Santiago, and

Detroit…The hell, I don't look when I drive. Am fed up. Don't discriminate. Well, I hate some of them, don't know why but do. Let them bother others, not me.

I'll also fight for my place, you'll see. The fighting's worse because of the pressure. Everybody telling me what to do. Entering school is pressure, walking the mall, watching the chicks go by is loaded with pressure…be careful, look out what you do, don't date immediately, keep hands off, as if everybody is dangerous to everybody, no joke.

Steve

Yeah. That's society made by adults—whether you like it or not. Can you make a choice, a selection? I don't see that.

Nick

Well, I told you, I fought. Not for nothing. I can't stand those pressures. Makes me feel bad and think dark. So we choose ourselves, how to do things, how to behave. Need no others. No Dad, he wouldn't understand, and tell me that our rules are identical to his…identical but slightly different. He'd say that the difference fades away with the years to come. What sarcasm.

Steve

No, not sarcasm but irony. Didn't he start somewhere?

Nick

That's OK for him, but none of my business. Our rules are my beginning. Could be the line of a poem. You write?

Steve

Of course, my diary. On a computer. No handwriting for me, my writing makes my thoughts inaccessible. Communicate my writings with people in my chat corner. On my web site. You too?

Dave

I feel the same, that type of writing gives you freedom, universal access. Password's privacy. Chat corners are my mirrors. Don't tell my sister, she needs a glass mirror to find her right image…

Steve

Mine told me that she stopped trying on her own body. Since she wants others to take her as she is, she likes herself.

Dave

Could be right. Feel often the same. It's difficult enough to accept yourself as you are, others should not make that more complicated…

Ritchie

But you may need correction or support of your image. Pressures how to act and when to care don't deliver.

Nick

That's exactly why I used my fists, to tell you again. We correct ourselves. That's our group, for as long as it exists. I like that now, I hate to think about tomorrow, don't even need that!

Images and Sounds

They "sing" the melody of "We are the champions…"

Ritchie

So sing loud: we are the champions…no: *we are our own society*!

Steve

Yeah! Loud. Have another beer.

Dave

We're our own society…

Steve

Who's there? You recognize that car, Dave? That's your Dad! Your Dad! How's that possible? Mine would never have stopped. Must I envy you, Dave…

Images and Sounds

Dave's father, a thirty-eight years old Wall Street lawyer, drives his Mercedes car along the group of friends. He recognizes his son Dave, hesitates, brakes and stops the car. Still behind the wheel, he takes his tie off and when he slowly gets out, he leaves his jacket on the backseat of the car. Walks to Dave and his friends, in shirt and jeans.

Dave

Dad! You stopped? You heard us singing? You did not have your radio on? What a surprise. So early today. Do you often take this route? Didn't know. Please knock before you enter. I'm here in my room!

Michael

Hi Dave. I wondered, at home there would perhaps not be so much time for a chat than at this incidental moment. Hello guys, nice to see you. Yes, I am Michael, Dave's father. You're expressing so much ease, free time, open space, nice air, I should perhaps envy you.

Dave

You could. However, consider this as our private ground and private conversations. We are not here for free floating thoughts or expressions. We debate, we fight with opinions and in doing so we enjoy our friendship. I had that in mind when I said "Knock", or "I'm in my room". You got it?

Michael

I do. In fact, I should leave you silently. Or turn around. Or should not have seen you. Or pretended to do so. But I don't like that. I know how there are two worlds here. I take the challenge. I don't want conflict, or an argument. I look for understanding, no more, no less.

Dave

I don't know whether I can speak for our group. But I appreciate your courage to stop and come to us. Must not be easy. Others may have a different opinion...

Nick

No, it's OK. Let him stay here. If he wants, he can listen. Might not be able to understand, or to talk. In any case not our way, no?

Steve

Let me tell you one thing, sir. Dave is one of us, and you're his father. So how can you be totally alien to us? That's against our bond of friendship, as long as it goes. Courageous to stop here. So I trust you, like I trust for instance my geography teacher. Is that enough? All agree? However,…

Nick

…indeed, we have to tell him what we were talking. If not, he can not communicate.

Dave

Yeah. There we go. We found, Dad, that one of the motives for our strong friendship is that we live under quite some pressure. You cannot imagine how strong social pressure is on us. All society tells us what *not to do:* no unsafe sex, no excessive drinking, dancing or disco, no cocaine or XTC, no drugs at all, no drinking and driving, no speeding, no discrimination, no sexual harassment, no guns, no violence, no civil…

Michael

…disobedience. A long list of "no's". Is that what causes pressures on you, the list of forbidden items? The apple in Paradise! I guess, in my days that list was even longer. Has there ever been a generation without such lists? Lists were a form of communication, the making of norms and values.

Nick

Well, the length of your list is not an issue for us. In your days! Bad argument! And what bad communication. You came away with it. You're an established lawyer now. We'll also achieve and come to good or even better jobs. My old Nissan is just the beginning. It will be different, anyway. The point is that you adults have only the "no's" listed for us. You are not at home when it comes to formulating issues positively. That's why friendship and togetherness is so important to us. We formulate and find the positive issues together. Our norms, only an umbrella for the pressures. Call our friendship self-protection. I would not mind.

Michael

I think I understand. Adults have often the same feeling. Many adult groups protect against too strong social norms in general. They are Freemasons, Rotarians, Members of Religious Groups, they adhere political parties or serve specific communities. The same feelings, a search for sharing and also for recognition…

Dave

…and a lot of pressure. Moral pressure. The pressure of stupidity such as: "Come with us and we tell you what to do, how to feel, how to think. If you do, you'll be happy and satisfied!" Moral consumer protection. Just like TV ad's. We hate that pressure. Our friendship is enough to make us go. Even in school. *Belonging* is the pressure we accept. Through our belonging, we'll make it, I guess. Don't forget how social scientists once started to observe us as a *peer group*. Peers are originally nobleman, you know! Belonging gives us the feeling of nobility. That's it. Laugh! But understand!

Steve

What is more: peer groups are adult-free, like our Internet corners. You're an exception, here and now!

Michael

A lesson. Well formulated, perfectly understandable. But why this negative emotion? Why a contrast to…let me say: your home, or even your school class?

Dave

Dad, be honest: how many hours are you for us at home? When are you at home? How many hours a day, a weekend? We already talk longer now than we did on one other day of this month! You adults are absent; so we find our belonging somewhere else, and create our guidelines, which you do not offer.

Steve

This here is sort of home. I spend more time here and at school then at home. 'Our' house? I don't know. Yeah, home is where I plug in! The Virtues Of The Net. Not of my parents. Don't worry, we'll make it. Good friends are few. We found some, for the time being. That'll do it.

Dave

Dad, you with your work and social obligations, Mom and her circles, work, education of the kids and all those things—you simply can not compete with our group. You cannot be as direct and understanding, speak the same language, have the same body as we do! So take it and leave it!

Michael

Only one thing. Your isolationism worries me. All this is not your own invention, nor a final solution for your specific problems. Your group is an expression of social norms as other life forms you criticize. Adults also hide away in small groups, they also do it for drinking, discussing, setting norms and many other issues that you mentioned. You would be more "normal" if you would not be so proud of your "exclusivity".

Dave

Well, we need that exclusivity. That's it!

Images and Sounds

Change of the scene.

We are in the room of Rachel, sister of Dave. Rachel is 13 years of age, an 8th grader. Her friend Maria, same age, same class, is with her. Both will soon finish Middle School.

The room is full of photographs—portraits of male sports figures, stars, musicians. Many and various mirrors, a small and overloaded make-up table.

Bed sheets and other items all pink colored.

Rachel

I like to try many clothes. It's as if I change identity with them. All those colors and shapes, you know. Dave would say it does not matter. For me, it does. One color, one shape is mine and not someone else's! So I have to try many. For how long? I don't know. I like the experiment. I like that because it makes me look older, and more mature. Would like to be fifteen, those girls are so different…when I see them, I see myself when I'm older. Are others a mirror to oneself?

Maria

See your future? A future will always be different. Like your body—one day, this jeans fit perfect, the next month it will be three inches to short. Changes. Always, everywhere! Like my mood. Need an anchor?

Rachel

My anchor man? (*Laughs*) Don't have yet. Sometimes, Dave gives me stability and plays that role.

Maria

My friends do the most of it. We all change, but we wish to stay together, to connect, to belong, to fit in…that's what makes us go.

Rachel

Correct. Belonging is what makes your identity, even where your own body does not seem to fit, friends do. I am not looking for a surrogate family. I can talk to Dave, to my Mom, to you and to other schoolmates. But what makes me feel stable is fashion, hairstyle, make up, clothes. Knowing your place at the pecking order in school is important. To become embraced. To lose, eventually. *Losers* confirm the importance of being *in*. No 'us' without 'them' who do not make it! Hate the thought of being a *loser* myself! Don't tell me that the world is full of losers and winners. Dad would say that. I'm not interested. I have to live now and here. Nowhere else.

Maria

Dave told me about your Dad. Think it's great how he stopped his car and went to the guys that late afternoon. He cares, I guess. Maybe the wrong way, but he does. He told Dave's friends that adults have the same need for friendship and belonging as we have. They also meet in social groups and spend their time to establish moral support. So, if they do the same as we do, why are they critical to our peer groups, our life-style as designed by ourselves?

Rachel

I don't know. Perhaps because their groups fit in their social pattern. They think that our does not, or keeps distance to their society…They nevertheless need their groups badly. I can see that when Mom leaves for visits, or comes home after such events. Belonging is important to everyone, I guess. Only the forms may be different.

Maria

Are they really?

Rachel

Well…they *look* different, in any case!

Maria

OK, but what is more important, the *look* or the *importance*?

Scene 2:
Family Talk: The Power of Belonging

Images and Sounds

We are again in the room of Rachel, the sister of Dave. Her room is full of photographs—portraits of male sports figures, film stars, musicians. Many mirrors, and a small, overloaded make-up table. Pink bed sheets and other items. Maria just left the room.

Her mother Esther, 36 years of age, is now with her. They drink a soda in Rachel's room.

Rachel is seated on her bed, the mother on a small stool. A comfortable and 'official' chair in the room remains unoccupied.

Rachel

…you think that friendship has to last for quite some time in order to be really friendship? Is a good and deep friendship after knowing each other, let me say, two days or three, impossible? You really think that? Dave told me more than once the opposite!

Esther

That's perhaps your feeling, yes.

Rachel

Can you explain?

Esther

Difficult. Has to do with my broader view on life. Friendship is a very important issue in each life, not to mention love relations. They develop, you know. They need time to develop. One should water them, like plants—and only after some time, they show their first blossoms.

Rachel

Wow! So romantic, Mom. Never known you were such a soul!

Esther

Well, Rachel, it may seem romantic, but the issue itself is not. I would say that it is not realistic and romantic to believe the opposite, as you do. You say, the friendship of a day holds perhaps for life. That's romantic, because it is the story of the Beautiful Prince, which awakens you and gives you life. A good relation is the product of labor of both partners, of finding out and being together for some time...

Rachel

So you and Dad would not accept when I would fall in love and—let us say—want to marry my lover a month later?

Esther

I would tell you again how all relations need time to grow. Sometimes they even do not grow at all; sometimes they are planted without roots or soil. You then have to take the consequences. At your age, I would not accept—you're too young.

Rachel

I feel that also. But hypothetically spoken, you do not feel that you disregard my autonomy in that case?

Esther

No, certainly not at your age or even later in your development. You are at the beginning of what should be the heart of your journey into life. We should take care that this journey...

Rachel

Mom, I'm not travelling, I am alive!

Esther

Correct. I am glad you say so. However, I am as much aware as you are, that your actual life situation as a 13 years old adolescent is loaded with contrasts and contradictions. That's not theory, that's our practice of living with you from day to day. You are not to blame for anything, but one moment you are a young lady, the other a teeny bopping. I like that, it's unique, and we love you for that. But your autonomy grows like your teeth, and one needs a dentist from time to time! No way out!

Rachel

But Mom, please don't disturb! This place where you are now, is given to me by you and Dad; it means everything to me. My life is like my room: received from you, OK, but extremely meaningful specifically to me!

Esther

…and to us. Believe that! To us also. I could not imagine to become estranged from you. However, our belonging together differs from year to year, from birthday to birthday, even from hour to hour! That's what I call 'growth', and hence my comparison to the life of plants.

Rachel

Listen! I hear someone coming home.

Must be Dave, Dad is never so early. Who else is climbing the stair so swiftly…Dave, are you there? We are here! You look so disturbed. What is going on? Are you OK?

Why home at this time of the day?

Dave

Hey there! Did you see Dad? He is not home? I phoned his office, but he was not there either. Might be in the Court Library, Ashley said to me with her secretarial overtones…

Esther

Why do you need Dad so urgently that you come home for it, after phoning the office? You know that we do not interfere with visits nor phone the office frequently…

Dave

No Mom, but…

Esther

What "but"? What causes you to break such a rule?

Dave

Well, Steve, you know Steve, don't you? Steve has a nice old Ford and at lunchtime he had a minor accident with that car. Bumped into a motorbike rider, no wounds but damage to the bike…apart from his car, of course. I wondered if Dad could say something about Steve's liability in this case, because the bike driver was furious and threatened to send a lawyer to his parents…

Esther

Steve may have been imprudent. Driving too fast or negligent. Were you there when it happened? No? So, why hold to Steve so strongly? Dad is not a lawyer for traffic accidents, you know that. Look at his web site!

Dave

But if we can help! Steve is my best friend, you know. He is one of us—we share rules, views, opinions, schoolwork, bad luck and setbacks, we speak the same language, we wear each other's clothes…

Rachel

Good you do not use each other's make up!

Dave

Shut up, you! What nonsense. You're too young to…

Esther

Please stop, Dave, stop. We can wait for Dad, he told me that he would come home early today. He might even be willing to phone or to receive Steve. But he cannot take the case, if it comes to that!

Dave

Mom, it might not come to that! But you have to understand, our solidarity…we were together for such a long time. These days, things start to change, I guess. Most of the friends begin dating chicks. That's different.

Rachel

How, why is that different?

Dave

I'm not going to tell you what a stupid question that is! Last year, we were so closely together, Ritchie, Nick, Steve and myself. We could speak about literally everything, sex, drugs, teachers, lesson contents, cloth, cars, money, but now it is as if especially Steve, but also others begin to reach out beyond our group. He sails away, going places, talking without us, dating or pretending to date. I can't say I don't like it, but everything starts to change so much. Feels weird.

Esther

So your urgent request that Dad helps Steve is your attempt to still keep close ties with him?

Rachel

Would you say you don't like that your friends date girls?

Dave

How can I answer? To be honest, it's rather difficult to comment on your questions. I would not like to loose Steve's friendship, and dating girls changes or even threatens the coherence of our group.

Esther

So you find yourself quite dependent on the group, Dave. You spoke in such tones to Dad, the other day. And now the same issue comes up. You're fighting the inevitable, which is called "change" in life! You feel challenged by that apparent change, so to say. Also challenged to change yourself, and add to your personal strength. Your peer group changes, and appears less reliable than before. A difficult phase to be in, that's very true!

Dave

You are very right. Do you know what worries me most? Pressures. This change of orientation within the group is another pressure—a pressure to not rely entirely upon those who were for quite some time your environment, your life world. In that case, I feel the eyes of others on me, where the group protected me, I feel more visible, more naked now. You know very well how they speak about us. Adolescents are lazy, egocentric, impolite, drug users, smokers, drinkers, without values, and the like…but I am not, and do not want to be. But how escape from such judging eyes of all others?

Esther

I understand. Among adults, we would say: "be yourself". However, most of us can not, that's the problem and people visit a shrink for it. Do not forget that "the judging eyes of others" as you said with an eloquence that must be in your genes, already have their profile of you as a member of your peer group. Not such a noble profile, as I read the other day in a leading magazine. You're said to show a lying and cheating standard behavior in the group, to have a religious canon like a salad bar: pick and choose, you're said to be prejudiced, discriminating, having an overtly ambitious attitude as far as jobs or family life are concerned…

Rachel

Mom, please, what a list. Must be for boys, for elder boys. I do not recognize any of these features. Neither would any of my friends be able to…

Esther

You're right, Rachel. Your peer group is still in tact, is a girls group and not yet showing any signs of dissolution. Dave's is different. He's confronted with rather serious and new challenges, you not. Maybe never.

Dave

Nice of you to read such magazines and not to tell me…Nevertheless, I feel that our group is different and does not belong to such general observations. You position me in between two pressuring profiles. You think I do not want to belong to any of the two. That's also right. But it does not do away with the importance of belonging…you can imagine. Especially with values. Where to find them?

Images and Sounds

Michael entered the house already some moments ago. Nobody paid attention because of the intense conversation. He refers to that immediately, feeling that it is important to be there.

Michael

Now I enter the family reunion in our daughter's private mansion! I was already in the house for some time. Nobody welcomed me, nobody even noticed. Great. You were so immersed in your conversation. Dave, I overheard you want to find what, where, and why do you need to find it?

Dave & Rachel

Hi Dad! Great you are there! Are you really in the mood to talk, not to just pass by?

Esther

Michael! We had a long discussion on many topics. Share with us!

Dave

But Dad, first of all I have to ask you for legal help...

Michael

You need legal help? For what? Have a problem?

Dave

No, Steve has! You remember Steve when from the other day. He bumped with his Ford into a motor bike, and the driver started to make problems with his liability. Now we both would ask you, what we should do. His parents are not lawyers, they don't know anything better than phoning their insurance guy. Could you perhaps simply listen to his story, and indicate what to do?

Michael

Here you are! That's my longtime theory. In the company of lawyers and physicians you feel safe! It's even not a joke. Tell Steve to make an appointment via Ashley. If he hesitates to come to the office, we can talk at the same street crossing we met before! No problem for me. Just let me know his preference. Let him bring his insurance papers and everything else we might need.

Dave

You're great, Dad. Thank you. Steve's dad would never have said so. Yes, papers, all the time papers…As soon as one gets in touch with you, one needs papers. That's the first requirement of the legal institutions, it seems.

Michael

You learned your lesson well. Papers and paperwork. When I entered Law School, nobody ever explained how legal work is paperwork packed in an institution as it were. We should learn to respect specific frames of thought and action or conduct of law as an institution. A lawyer is not free to *read* his documents, laws, rules or declarations and decisions the way he wants or can. He works in a framework of meanings, which are determined in advance by the established institution.

Dave

Does this not change you into a machine? In other words, is the legal representation of life events not a manner to cheat people? But before you go on, tell me precisely, *what is an institution?* I hear that word so many times, please tell Rachel and me what that is!

Michael

Not easy to answer. An institution is, let me say: *a peer group in adult society.* Individuals always have to live and work in groups. One cooperates with others, one has a shared need for instruments, for administrative or other provisions, one can only work and live a professional life in an ensemble of persons, devices, goods, opinions, ends and means. Such types of relation provoke what peers also do. They prescribe how to behave or what to think, they format social life and constitute a form of power. It's when you say that someone acts 'typical', for instance a 'typical' dentist, lawyer, economist, physician, nurse...represents and became a specific pattern of behaviors and beliefs that reaches far beyond any individual's life!

Dave

So you sacrifice freedom when you enter your job. You *become* your job, with all its properties and specifics. Our peer groups give us freedom and do not take that freedom away. On the contrary, they are the *we* that act by means of our individual selves...

Michael

Don't forget that your peer group gives the freedom to act within the limits that the group, the *we*, accepts. You're free because of those limits—look at your cloth, your idiom, your norms, your behavior. The same for me, when I act as a lawyer, or for Mom when she is family member, or Rachel as sister in a family or an 8th grader in a Middle School…From each of us, one can read the properties of the institution we live in. I feel clearly, how I am whistled back at the moment I move outside the legal institution! Law constructed legal institutions that whistle you back, for instance the Supreme Courts. Such Courts do not only decide a case or review a decision, they also re-define the limits of law within which I am allowed to operate. No, you can never do what you want as an individual. Effective legal action is very limited although it goes to the entirety of life! Steve and you experience that soon, I guess.

Rachel

It means you have to be careful all the time, like a surgeon, a nurse or an Alan Greenspan, who's opinions are immediately causing highs and lows in the stock market?

Michael

A good example. Schools seldom explain the impact of institutions on individuals and how behavior results from institutional frameworks. So you adolescents are helpless and hopeless once confronted with the specifics of an institution. That's the reason why Steve wants to speak with me! It's his uneasiness with the law, as it would be with medical, economic or political issues. People are not trained in that regard. But I think *institutions* was not the issue of your talk with Mom and Rachel when I entered?

Esther

True. I am glad you'll cooperate. However, the story with Steve is not a purely legal matter. Dave feels that Steve and other friends do longer stick to the exclusivity of their peer group. Some develop other interests, for instance when dating girls. Dave tends to defend the group's coherence because it is important to him. I said how he's apparently in a process of change, a change that defies his feelings of identity. He's now in an 'in-between' position, a difficult one.

Michael

Wow, Esther, what a clear insight! You agree, Dave? I am happy we can talk about it.

Dave

Well, I hesitate to disrupt your optimism. Mom is not wrong, she is also not right in her observation. It's understandable enough to me that our group changes. That has tremendous consequences, as if I must leave one family for another.

Esther

Would that solve your problem? Find another family, another *we*? Like the little kids story: 'if you do not like what we say, try other parents…'

Dave

No, the problem is not only on identity. My friends and myself built a pattern of *values*. They are expressed in our cloth, in our drinking habits, in our attitude in class, in our vocabulary, our views on society at large…If that orientation disappears now, where do I find another?…

…on the Internet, perhaps? Many of us do try indeed! With other friends? Tell me how to find them. Teachers, text books in school, periodicals, magazines perhaps? Very abstract. You, the family circle? I am the only one here that has my age, my views, my body, my attitudes. *I'm lonely here*! And pressured by the many dominating prescriptions—you have no idea what I have to do and not to do, I told you. I'm lonely here, and that is the threatening perspective!

Michael

Let me try another word. You are not *lonely* here: you are *unique* here, with us...

Dave

...I feel that uniqueness as loneliness. One of a twin, the other unknown and absent.

Michael

...sounds terrible, but is that not the counterpart of belonging? How can one appreciate belonging without experiencing what it is to *not* belong?

Dave

Don't start philosophical, please.

Michael

No, I'm not. I am happy that you talk with us. Not many of you guys do that. What you say emphasized the importance of our belonging as a family. I don't mean a statement about the "values of family life". I'm talking about the reality that we are. Are you aware what a minority we are, we the "father-mother-kids"—family? And what a minority a "family-that-talks/communicates" is today?

Rachel

What does that mean? What importance has it for Dave's feelings, which one day might become mine also?

Esther

I guess it means a lot. In other words, whatever happens to your or Dave's peer groups, we are there—as long as life is given to us. You are not without a basis and do not need to live without a basic trust! Was that not the subject of our conversation?

Michael

Indeed, Esther. It's not only about us. You guys often forget how there are many forms of belonging that provide a basic trust. It's critical that they do not always do. Think of one-parent families, of parents/grandparents and other multigenerational families, of same sex families, of parents with adopted children, or with genetically 'own' children together with adopted kids. They all are one form or another of 'belonging', beyond any 'natural' order or instinct.

Esther

That is life, and also a perfect description of your peer group. Belonging seems to me a social form that reaches beyond natural order. No matter whether you call it 'family' or 'friendship' or 'peers', it is always 'belonging'. Adults can learn from both of you how important that is.

§3 PEER GROUPS:

Part II: "STORIES"

Scene 1:
"The Story of Stories"

Images and Sounds

The noises and voices of a normal school building. Students going in and out. Some hang around, others talk, and some have a soda, some books. A small classroom door is half-open. One can see two teachers at one of the tables. Sketches and phrases are written on the blackboard, several desktops are not yet closed.

Mario (28 years of age) and Ben (29 years of age) are two teachers. They had a group of students at work with Part I of "Peers". Within thirty minutes, they expect several of these students to come back.

Mario

I wonder how many of the students liked that first Part.

Ben

You mean, those who were in the "Peer Groups" for the first time? All others are already hooked up! Steve: Good grief! "Hooked up" means having casual sex.

Mario

Yes, students might ask what the point of the story is, and how the story unfolds. Do they recognize its links to their own situation? They will certainly find many phrases and manners of speech that are theirs, but the attitude of Dave and Rachel's parents could disturb them. Not all parents react the way Michael and Esther do. When Michael stopped his car at the crossing, I saw bewilderment on the faces of some students. They wondered if their own Dad would have reacted that way.

Ben

Yes, the point of the story! That's the issue...

Mario

What do you mean? The point of the story, its essence, or its most important issue is...a normal question, no?

Ben

Seems to be. But is that so? I often doubt whether all our stories have a real point, an essence, a most important issue. Or are we just acting *as if* they have such a point, for I don't know what reason—I don't know.

Mario

Ben, you're starting to talk like a philosopher. How can you make the distinction between "doing as if" and "doing"? That's a very old and puzzling question, you know. Is your question whether everything might only be a 'doing as if'? I would not like to discuss that with the students!

Ben

Why? You mean to say it leads to nihilism? To something without a guarantee that we live in a *common* world when we *communicate* with others?

Mario

Sure Ben. I'm saying you scare me!

Ben

You're a bit too fast, Mario. For me, the question is how we construct a reality that accommodates our lives. We do that when we tell our stories. I tell you, "Listen, what happened to me last night. I was...and then, and then...and now! What's your opinion?" is what you can hear all the time. We live a story-telling life!

Mario

I guess you want to sell me the idea that we should discuss and understand *reality as a form* of life and experience? Without further ado?

Ben

Mario, it's your turn to be philosophical! Yes, I want to sell you that idea, yes, and sell it to all the others.

Mario

Why? Life is difficult enough, and our students have enough worries, questions, ambiguities, and pressures.

Ben

Why? We provide our students the skills to express themselves appropriately within our social frameworks. However, they should above all understand how one is always expected to obey the requirements that pertain to the continuation of our society, as concealed in our story telling communication…

Mario

…you suggest that our students must understand how all story telling, their 'communication' and 'interactivity' included, is in essence a form of practicing social norms?

Ben

Yes. When we speak, we sustain the basic issues and their images that altogether form the reality of our lives.

Mario

I don't understand you. Don't social scientists call that 'constructivism'? Do you suggest that the words we speak are not only a means of communication, but create a common image of reality in which we live? Is that what you meant to say? Is this not what the poets have been saying for thousands of years?

Ben

Sure enough, but we forgot about the poets and did not listen to the scientists who operated the same way…we defamed their scheme of thoughts in the past centuries as 'poetic', and 'not scientific'. Today, we appreciate the poets anew, and perhaps say they're not radical enough! Disturb the surface appearance of a phrase, an expression, a color—and you feel a conflict of norms or of values that rule everybody's life.

Mario

Gosh! I never saw it that way. So you want to say that our saying "Hello!" or "Hi" or "Bye" or "…re you doing today?" are not only *expressions* but also *norms*? The use of an expression is the fulfillment of a norm, you mean? Wow, great insight.

Ben

Correct. There is more. See how modern culture is rooted in images, in films, TV, also scanners, space images and images of cells, screen representations, text books full of diagrams, pictures and the like, you name it! They're the reality we live in. Create images all the time. Interaction and interactivity, or the stories we tell are no exception.

Mario

Aren't you suggesting that we basically live within sets of stories which we repeat all the time? An understanding of what we say and communicate is in recognizing those repeated schemes? *Are the peer groups of our students not perfect "recognition machines"?*

Ben

"I am here for the opposite. Say 'open up' and I am with you! How comes that you like your experiences to be packed in the conventionalized narrative, with its opening, its middle, its nicely balanced ending? Before you even open your mouth, your language will comfort everybody, will disregard any criticism, and will deliver a safety that is the ultimate drowsiness..." *Do yourself a favor, wake up to your mind.* I forgot what group of the early seventies had that song, may have been the Beatles, I don't remember. But it's just that, just that!

Mario

And what about the *institutional* issues in the Peer Groups program?

Ben

His own kids questioned Michael about this issue, you remember. He had difficulties answering because he did not or could not see how institutions are always speaking the language of "the opening, the middle, the nicely balanced ending"! Institutions are perhaps the most important form of life, because they organize our social relations in accordance with those patterns of story telling. We must deliver exactly *that* insight! *If you are not trained to understand your own words, you're lost.* You simply repeat the norms and forms of the institution, and do not bear any personal responsibility. Your drowsiness...

Mario

I do not understand. How and why? And what about *Peers*?

Ben

Wasn't it said in the first Part how especially adolescents are helpless once they enter our institutions? Why are they helpless and lost? Because they don't have the skills to understand institutions. *Institutions—Their Opening Phrase:* "Sir, Young man, who are you and what are you here for?"—as if everybody knows the purpose of his or her life! As if everybody possesses full awareness about his or her identity! *Their Middle Phrase:* "Miss, Young Lady, tell me everything, why, when, and how…"—as if all our stories, narratives and experiences are rational, clear, and can be reconstructed at any moment! *Their Ending Phrase:* "So now, thanks to our intervention, everything is like it always was before the catastrophe or the Unexpected Event took place!" As if life is a constant attempt to get over surprises, shocks, sudden events, as if everything can be repaired in life, all problems always solved—that's what our institutions are for. Sleep well, they say, we'll solve your problems! Look at Courts, Hospitals, Consultation Rooms, Stock Markets, Police Stations, and Civic Centers…!

Mario

So, you say, if you only repeat the conventional forms of narration, you don't really speak! Your "you" is concealed, it cannot take responsibility! Is that what you…

Ben

Sure, and that goes also to peers! Is it not universally known that peer groups are in the first place what I'll call *speech communities*? Whether they concern four friends or ten members, a Public Service Community or a Secret Society—it does not matter. Speech always does the trick! Of course, the Service Community is not a peer group, but such an institution functions in very much the same way…let me come back to what I said before. Peer groups create a reality to live in. They master the reality of life! It's always the *we* that counts. Adolescents need peer groups more than adults. That's clear. Adolescents are in the process of an orientation towards our world and develop social skills at a distance to that adult world. However, that distance will shrink year after year, rapidly, smoothly, thanks to their peer groups which helped them to bridge many gaps…

Images and Sounds

Students come in the classroom, disturb the conversation, and walk to the computers to open the programs again. They have apparently no idea of the subject of Ben and Mario's conversation.

Mario, to Ben

If I look at their faces, I wonder how I can make this clear to them. Yet it should become a substantial part of their life! It all looks so very different now, Ben. You agree?

Ben

I do!

Scene 2:
"Sunset Boulevard"

Images and Sounds

After the lessons of Ben and Mario, Dave entered the classroom. He is one of the 'pioneers' of the program, and knows Ben and Mario very well. Dave, after the two teachers closed their computers and room, jumps in Ben's car. The two go for a walk to the coast, a few miles away. Ben agreed to bring Dave home later.

Ben

Nice weather today. It was a pity to stay in the classroom for such a long time. You really do not know whether it is winter of summer, once you are inside. Many times I feel as if the educational work is abstract and taking place in closed rooms.

Dave

…and in closed circuits.

Ben

Correct, if I understand you well. What a claim about communication in education settings!

Dave

I associate education with classrooms, halls, special event rooms, with groups in school, in community centers, civic centers, churches, reserved places in gardens, parks, lawns or woods, with special groups, organized visits and excursions, an industry of closed events. Ben, where is there a symbol of free air, open space, infinite exchange, where are there horizons rather than precise goals, growth rather than prefabricated achievement?

Ben

I never saw it that way!

Dave

Look at their architecture. You don't see it?

Ben

What?

Dave

A premeditated commonness under safe roofs!

Images and Sounds

Sounds of traffic, from inside the car. One can see a row of nice houses, special architecture. Trees and great gardens, lanes leading to main entrances.

Ben

Well said. What else can we do? Do you know better? Look to your right at the beautiful houses over there! They must date from the end of the eighteenth century—a treasure in this young country. Some seem to have their original colors. It must be great to live there, how different from the spirit you sketch out. What to do? Do away with it all, and introduce the spirit of Montessori, or have schools in the open air, winter and summer?

Dave

They exist. Didn't change anything!

Ben

You mean what?

Dave

Teachers should not dominate as if they have to do so by nature. Organize as many groups as students like. Create forms of dialogue. Introduce co-assignment in large groups. Change classrooms as often as needed. Fresh air is what we need. Dialogues. Not always hourly schedules, textbooks without interactive features, prefabricated achievements.

Ben

Aren't you too much influenced by your peer group experiences? I know how important they are to adolescents. But we cannot re-organize our educational system in accordance with peer group structures!

Dave

Why not?

Ben

You would never grow up! Always stay in the same group related patterns.

Dave

"Never become an individual" you'd like to say. Should we not come out of the peer group like we must come out of the womb? I once read that line!

Ben

In a way…yes!

Dave

You suggest that the model of my educational ideal is the peer group. However, it would be quite generally accepted if I said that the model should be the family…

Ben

Is there a lot of difference?

Dave

Yes, insofar as they speak the same language, share equal interests, often also share values and norms, have a comparable awareness about learning. They form an interactive community. That's important to each of them. Moreover, they are trained—it's the nature of that method—to become a bit self-interrogating and reflective.

Ben

I thought peer groups have a different level of awareness, especially about society around them…

Dave

True. They also have more intensive face-to-face contacts. I spent more time in my peer group than in my family, despite the great attitude of Mom and Dad. Even TV watching at home, or sleeping there, has its effects and feedbacks in the group. Don't forget that we act as individuals in school, in the family, in civic center activities and the like. You always act there as one individual person. Not in my group. *We* feel as one person. You know, we often change names…

Ben

I don't understand. You mean…

Dave

…correct. In the group I have a different name. *Dave* has become *Swingy*, from the David & Goliath story, my father would not like to hear that; *Steve* is called *Stable*, and so forth. They give us a different identity—could never be the case in schools, or in the family. I once said I was lonely in the family, the only one of my age, views, problems, feelings.

Ben

What was the reaction?

Dave

Dad answered I'm unique in the family. What a difference! It does not emphasize the difference between *Dave* and *Swing,* you know. Problems of transition are problems of identity, I read in one of the books in our Civic Center. I guess the author had no idea about the reality of his phrase.

Images and Sounds

Traffic signs indicate more than one road to the coastal roads. Noises of cars and music form a radio.

Ben

We're near the coastal road. You see that sign? I think I'll go left now, to avoid most of the traffic. I'd like to get out of the car soon. We came for a walk, not a ride.

Dave

Didn't you tell us once, that one can never perceive or study the fly in the eye? You need distance to the object in your eye to know that there is something in your eye. The same is true for our group. We move a distance from society, school, or family and consider what we want to achieve in that society. Achievers we are, sometimes lonely achievers…Our peer groups are providing the space to consider…and to discuss. Didn't you once speak about our group as a speech community? The best expression I've ever heard!

Images and Sounds

Ben and Dave drive the Coastal Road slowly down. A beautiful sunset is imminent, but that will take about half an hour. At a nice parking place, directly going to the sea, Ben stops his car. The two get out, and walk down to the shore. It looks like a nice walk. Sounds of the sea, some wind, hardly any other visitors.

Ben

This is beautiful. Let's get out here. We have so much to talk about, and there is so much to see. In half an hour we'll see a magnificent sunset. After that, we'll walk back and drive home. OK with you, Dave?

Dave

This is indeed great. How difficult to talk about our issues and perceive all this beautiful landscape. For me, it's often difficult to perceive the sea as a landscape. Trick of our semantics, of course.

Ben

…and of our training. We're trained to associate landscape with trees and hills, fields and pastures, not with the surface of water, not with the immensity of that ocean. Associations are mainly a cultural product, you know. They go from your taste to your judgment, from your perception to your semantics. They're everywhere in our personality, a culture in itself.

Dave

I have the feeling that the main subject of our conversations is the *peer experience*. When I talk about that and you ask me, it is as if we cannot share that experience, as if I speak another language and have to find metaphors to clarify…don't forget that peer groups concern an entire lifestyle, an attitude that embraces all major issues of modern life. For instance, peer groups sustain a great diversity of political views. Issues pertaining to sex, to violence, to marginal behavior are included. Not all peer groups are school groups; not all school groups support adult identity…

Ben

Tell me about a secret of peer life, which is in the coherence between sex and violence. Of course, in theories on human sexuality, in texts of Freud for instance, the two are often seen together. I didn't know that peer groups also go for that combination.

Dave

I think you pose the wrong question or rather: you formulate the question wrong. Let's walk over there, on the top of the dune. We may have a good sunset view.

Ben

You teach me, so tell me how to pose the right question, Dave.

Dave

Yuck! To see such relations between violence and sex is an adult approach. Our concern in our peer group is different. It does not involve any type of practicing sex together with any form of violence. The two are seen as mighty forces in our life, adolescent as well as adult which have to become mastered, tamed, controlled. Our major point is how to gain control over these vital forces in our life! That may differ from your adult views. These views of yours are from the standpoint of *already having* sexual experiences, and *having met* all sorts of violence. Ours is from *before* one has such experiences. *How do you become*…that's the issue, you know…we become a 'somebody', don't forget! Our groups help us in that regard. More than any family life can ever do!

Ben

Dave, you're great. We now must climb that little dune, and watch. What you say brings me delete to new insights, really!

Dave

Ben, I must tell you that you forgot a lot of things since you grew up. Let me raise a question. What is the difference between a 'gang' of adolescents and a 'peer group'?

Ben

I am sorry, I do not know. Must be a sociological item, this difference…

Dave

No, Ben! You did not listen to me. I said it already in other words. "Gangs' often *practice* the unholy combination of sex and violence. 'Peers' help to *master* it. The behavior of gang members is legally reprehensible and many citizens think, for that reason, that gang members are important in juvenile life. What is more important: the learning to master, or the brute exercise of reprehensible behavior? For you, the answer is clear, but it is not an issue to many of your colleagues…

Images and Sounds

Sounds of the sea, some night wind coming. Light breeze. Clear sunset.

Ben

Look at what happens before our eyes! Is it not beautiful, worth the driving up here? Are beauty of nature and beauty of human creations, of art…

Dave

Ben, don't talk now, don't philosophize. Look! Is looking not sufficient for all of us? Overwhelming? A gift, perhaps?

Ben

Dave, you are so right. Let's be silent and look.

Images and Sounds

One can see the two sitting at the top of a dune, watching the sunset, silently. Hardly any sounds. After some time, the sun has set and it starts to become dark. The two get up and walk in the direction of the car.

Ben

Today I learned a lot from you, Dave.

Dave

Thanks for telling me. There is yet so much to come for me…One thing about sex and violence I must add. You should understand that I did not talk about the content of the two, about how we practice sex or violence. In fact, in our peer groups, which differ from gangs, the action is not the issue. It is rather the learning. Exercising violence, also in combination with sex, is not the rule for our groups. Learning that there is violence, that there is sex, that there is rape and abuse of alcohol combined with violent behavior is the issue as well as learning how to cope with those forces. Do you understand, it's about *learning*.

Ben

Is there not a tremendous difference in that regard between girls and boys?

Dave

Sure. Nick, one of our group once reminded us how he had to fight to enter our group. Even ours, the most peaceful and civilized group you can imagine! What we do with our fists, girls most frequently do with words. They can be nasty with their stories, very nasty.

Ben

So, my idea about peers as a speech community is not irrelevant?

Dave

Not at all! You should elaborate this idea. Gossip is deadly, especially where it goes in between the rows of a classroom. No matter whether it is about a teacher, a student, students of other classes and the like…Fists, physical force, is more limited.

Ben

And you can limit force yourself, where those who initiate it cannot master gossip and other speech activity!

Dave

Well, that is particularly important for adolescents around my 15 years of age. We do not *practice* sexual activity that much, let alone violent behavior, but *talk* about it a lot, a lot. I guess we need the safety of the peer group talking first. Before we venture the action itself! Our dating is always on the basis of that earlier peer talk. Don't think it is directly related to family values, church, civic community, school or what institutions you mention. At its best it's indirectly related, through the filter of our group.

Ben

I understand. We're near your home now. Are you tired from all this talk? It's a lot. For me, it's great to hear all this from you; you know it will help me a lot to…

Dave

...that is the reason for telling you. I even told you secrets. I keep secret what secret I mean. Don't ask me, don't exploit me. I trust you.

Images and Sounds

They come to the entrance of Dave's house. It is pitch dark. The two stay in the car for awhile. First, the engine of the car is still on; later Ben turns the engine off.

Dave

...our issue is to live and to learn how to live. Some of us think life is coffee and beer until four in the early morning. Compensated for by sleeping until four in the afternoon. A weekend portion. Is that freedom? It's not the average of life, but certainly not its fulfillment, that's clear enough.

Ben

However, it is the fundamental reason for peer groups being so important to all of you. A public secret. You need friends and recognition; you need a good and warm group feeling. Only a few of you want to stay alone. Is that correct?

Dave

Yes, sure. What else?

Ben

Well, that could lead to a complete and overall profile of peer group functions. Your groups offer more or less durable social relations. They support you as a person, make informed choices possible and sustain your curiosity and exploratory behavior. They are an encompassing community, in particular based on a common language and on shared values. Are your groups not very hedonistic?

Dave

What do you mean? I don't understand!

Ben

All well and good! If I hear you, everything that goes to your peer group is connected to ideas and performances of "the good life"—to say it the way the Greek used to express themselves. Hedonism means that gaining pleasure might be the most important thing. Your individualism serves that purpose, your emphasis on learning how to behave, how to cope with the requirements of the free market, its liberalism, its interpretation of the family, the community, of church and school networks, not to mention other social support networks. You explained how deep and far this goes. The group is an exercise place for learning how to cope with sex and violence, how to enter in a world of gender differences, how to serve communities without being a loser…You see that there are always *values* at stake?

Dave

It's those values you want me to confront? You want to disclose them? I need to emphasize the peers' support function, not their help in the process of realizing these values.

Ben

I have to think about that.

Images and Sounds

Ben starts the engine of his car again. Dave makes a move to get out.

Ben

It brings our conversation back to the problem of how peers relate to the major social institutions. My question about the realization of values goes to that point. Are peer groups, when they fully function, really that different from other social institutions? Or are only 'gangs' different because of their initiation of all sorts of reprehensible behavior?

Dave

Ben, thanks for everything you have been thinking with me, asking, considering, showing your open mind. I'm tired and want to sleep. I guess peers and families complete each other, they are not very different in their structures. Both aim at the emergence of personal identity, but they may do that differently. They require us to play roles, often within other roles, which we will never play anymore in our lives. And, what is more, they teach us to cherish expectations. All this is indeed a matter of…story telling! That's correct!

Images and Sounds

Dave leaves the car and walks towards the house. Ben drives away. All is silent, all dark.

Scene 3
"The Blackboard"

Images and Sounds

Mario and Ben meet the next day in the classroom. Dave also enters, apparently to have another talk with Ben, knowing that Ben would have told Mario the outlines of yesterday's conversation between him and Ben.

Ben

Hi, Dave. Nice to see you again, "under the roof of the institution" as you suggested yesterday! Hope you slept well. It was a great view, last night, wasn't it? I spoke a bit about our talks with Mario, as you could presume.

Dave

Yeah!

Mario

I think it was great, you showed quite a bit of reflection…

Dave

Don't exaggerate, Mario. That's one of your virtues but also one of your vices! Perhaps genetics at work!

Mario

Touché! But tell me, what are we going to do with all your information, views, and opinions, especially when completing the Program we're in?

Ben

Let us not repeat or extend yesterday's conversations. We might come to no other result than the repetition of what already has been said. I feel the strong need for an outline of our issues and perhaps also a discussion about how to proceed. Students will not enter this classroom before 10.15 a.m., so we have nearly an hour. Let's use that time! Dave, please help us formulate and correct us where necessary.

Images and Sounds

The classroom and its blackboard. The three make notes, write words and concepts which they vaguely order by means of arrows, lines and borders.

Mario

I agree. Here is a piece of chalk and there's the blackboard. We could use it and wipe our writings out before the students arrive. Ben, what's your opinion?

Ben

I think it's a good solution. Let us postpone discussions until after our list is complete. It will in any case represent the best knowledge we have.

Dave

You guys talk creatively! Go on!

Ben

When I think back to all our conversations between Mario and me or Dave and myself yesterday night, I guess that there are *four* groups of issues. As far as I can see, the *first* are general and on the level of facts about peers. The *second* pertain to some opinions of peer groups. The *third* are on our personal approaches and the *fourth* on specified issues of importance. Given that investigation, we might find what more to do!

Mario

The proof of the pudding is in the eating. You go!

Ben

Let's start with general observations. I'll write down that the great majority of our adolescents spend most of their time in peer groups. Often more than in the family circle, if there is one!

Dave

True, and that is not dependent upon the quality of family life! It is so even where the family supports the adolescents and creates excellent relationships. I think that's important.

Ben

You said it! There is furthermore a clear distinction possible between *gangs* and *peers*. That's the second thing to write here. It's important in public debate; Dave made that clear in our conversation more than once. I write thirdly that emphasis in peer groups is on *talk* and not on *organized social action*. If the talk leads to action, then the action is mostly individual.

Mario

Last but not least, I would say—I was waiting for that to come—you must add that peer groups *filter* opinions, judgments, value orientations, expectations in the family, in church, school, community and related institutions. They have an important critical function in adolescent life, I would say.

Ben

So far, so good for the first group of observations. The second is on the questions that form an *opinion on peer groups*, especially among adults, parents and teachers.

Dave

Perhaps these are the most important issues of all. We often have the idea we're misjudged all the time! That's very frustrating, you know.

Ben

OK. Sure, I see two major questions. The *first* is here under "Major Questions". Are peer groups an alternative, perhaps supplementary to (for instance) family values, or are they autonomous, self-supporting and in competition with the family and other primary groups? You will understand that peer groups are judged very differently when they are perceived as an alternative or as autonomous and beyond communication.

Dave

You said it! I seldom experience the supplementary attitude; it's always adversity and hostility. That makes us shy, makes the group a secret one! You would perhaps say: a self-fulfilling prophecy. I once heard you saying that; it was correct, very correct.

Mario

Wonder about your *second* point, Ben. It must go to a more personal and psychological appreciation of the members of a peer group. The groups are said to have a bad influence on the kids. Write that in the same section.

Ben

Correct. What is more, adults live with the idea that peer members are prematurely independent. Their opinions on values such as sex, violence, gender, religion, on God, on life, on the environment and the like, become uncontrollable as soon as adolescents are living their peer life. They built a private language and become a loss for society at large.

Dave

Very realistic. I wonder what your *third* group of issues is!

Mario

OK. Consider that third group here on the blackboard; I call it "Relevance". The first is for me the importance of peer groups in adolescent life. I think we have to emphasize that importance. Students will feel appreciated by their membership of peers, and parents can quiet down their negative feelings.

Dave

Great! What are your arguments?

Mario

"Peer groups protect and guide the identity formation of young people, some 22 million US citizens"—that's not nothing! It is socially and politically not correct to neglect this fact or give it only a negative image. It's a matter of value orientation and of redefining the task of families whether one can appreciate this fact as a positive contribution to society at large.

Dave

I fully agree. That's great!

Ben

Let me write down here the capacity of peer groups to mediate values and norms. The social networks and the Internet do not directly influence adolescents but do so indirectly, through the mediation of peers. One should consider this important outbalancing of influences.

Mario

Sure, the adult-free character of peer groups does not imply they produce an adversary attitude or a negative influence, which one has to fight. Without peer groups, I think, family life would be absolutely different. It would require a comeback of agrarian structures, of organic family life where many generations live together. That's impossible to imagine in contemporary society.

Ben

We should furthermore unravel the social structures of peer groups. Peers are not uniform. They rather reflect the many faces of society at large. They are predominantly speech communities, and structured like other social institutions.

Dave

I can't believe my ears! Would you say that our peer groups are like school, church, family, or comparable social groups? Do you really mean to say that? Why then are they so important to us, why do you think we invest so much in having them, creating them, sustaining them, changing them?

Ben

Don't get nervous, Dave! We do not speak about *contents* but envisage *structures*. A structure is, as you know, about patterns of relationships. It is also about the various roles, powers, laws that arrange a social phenomenon. We precisely consider that pattern, shape, set of rules or system, and this time not any emotional, psychological or ethical contents. And certainly not your emotional experience with peer groups. You are correct: one should make that very clear in the course of the Program!

Mario

Our list is long. I have three more issues to investigate, as Ben already suggested. They come here on the blackboard. Ben might have more such issues. My first is that we must deal with gender issues. How do peer groups at various adolescent ages deal with gender? There is a clear difference between girls and boys. Then, there is the fact that gender is for a long time beyond the peer experience. Various coping strategies are talked about; their management is the subject of an ongoing conversation. Where dating starts, the firm structure of the peer group is threatened.

Ben

Add to all this in the same column that we do not possess a set of objective qualifications to judge peer groups either by their expressiveness, social value or ethical norms. They are what they are—their relations are facts, which cannot be judged by other facts.

Dave

That is an important point of view. We often struggle with it when people talk about our behavior. I know how many of us for instance take a magazine and have a quick look at it. We "read" the fashion photos, look quickly at their body language, the clothes and their postures, we "zap" the pages and "sip" its images. Now, don't come and ask whether I am an illiterate, or tell that I'm not able to read a magazine…

Ben

A good example. We might come back to it. We've no more time now. I expect the students' arrival any moment. Let's have a final and conclusive look at the blackboard's notes. Here's our blackboard:

I General Issues

a. Majority of adolescents live in peer groups.

b. Distinction between gangs and peers.

c. Emphasis on talk, on narrative activities.

d. Peers filter social influences of all kinds.

II Major Questions

a. Are peer groups autonomous or supplementary to families and other institutions?

b. Do peer groups have a bad influence on individual members?

III The Issue of Relevance

a. The importance of peer groups for identity formation.

b. The adult-free character does not imply an adversary attitude.

c. Peer structures include (1) a field of dominating speech activity, and (2) an internal organization like other social institutions.

IV Other Issues

a. Gender issues are complex and multi-layered.

b. Peers cannot be qualified by objective criteria.

c. The "reading" of social phenomena in peer groups has authentic features.

Ben

Great, this is a good list of issues for further analysis. There are at least two out-standing issues, the *institutional and narrative character of peer groups.* How shall we deal with them?

Dave

Well, pin it all down to one issue—an issue you mentioned many times before. If I understood you well, narratives are never beyond or without an institution, and institutions never without their specific narratives. An analysis of narratives, of stories, may be the key you are looking for. Is that what you wanted me to conclude? Give it a try!

§4 P E E R S

Part III: "CASES AND OTHER RIDDLES"

Scene 1:
"Family & Friendship"

Images and Sounds

In the classroom where Part II was situated, one can now see several students working on their computers. Others work with their personal web sites. The four friends whom we met in Part I, Dave, Nick, Steve, and Ritchie, are also present with Rachel, Dave's thirteen year old sister and her friend Maria, together with the teachers Ben and Mario. The latter takes the initiative.

Mario

We decided to offer you a different approach to the understanding of the fundamentals of Peer Groups as adults see them and as you experience them. We have the notes on the blackboard copied for you on your personal web sites, and you can always find them. It might even be easier to download them soon. A handwritten leaflet contains the essentials for the exercises to come. They are based on talks, observations, and the scanning of literature on "Peers". I now give that leaflet to all of you.

Images and Sounds

Mario hands out the following leaflet:

<u>ON PEER GROUPS</u>

<u>I General</u>

a. Majority of adolescents in Peer Groups.
b. Distinct Gangs and Peers.
c. Emphasis Narrative Activities.
d. Peers filter.

<u>II Major Questions</u>

a. Peer Groups: autonomous or supplementary?
b. Bad influence on individual members?

<u>III Relevance</u>

a. Peer Groups & Identity Formation.
b. Adult-free, not adversary attitude.
c. Peer structures include
(1) a field of speech activity, and
(2) an organization like other social institutions.

IV Further Issues

a. Gender differences.

b. Peers not qualified by objective criteria.

c. Specific "reading" of social phenomena.

Ben

We offer you furthermore a "case", a "story" from real life, which happened in the US in the mid 1980's. There are various questions in this story that you should relate to features on peer groups as written down on the handout. In other words, that list can help you to efficiently analyze the story. I've written the main questions on the next leaflet.

Ben hands out the following leaflet.

A story analysis in the Peer Groups Program

(a) Detect which **various forms of belonging** support people and determine the story of their lives. Peer groups experience a diversity of such forms of belonging.

Example:

Forms of belonging that support people could be: near—or far blood relations, friendships and peer groups, communities, religious groups.

(b) Understand how there is always a **variety of distances** in patterns of social relationships. There is for instance proximity and there is remoteness up to temporary alienation in human interrelations. Indicate such distances, if possible on a scale you construct for instance from 1 to 5.

Example:

FRIENDSHIP: 1—2—3—4—5: "2"

FAMILY: 1—2—3—4—5: "2 1/2"

LOVE: 1—2—3—4—5: "1"

(c) Make **profiles** of [1] **opinions,** [2] **attitudes** and [3] **motivations** of the individuals involved.

Example:

[1] Most individuals value friendship less than love—I agree;

[2] Many develop a distant attitude to foreigners—I don't agree;

[3] Most adolescents want to achieve—Me too!

(d) Investigate what **institutions** are at work in the story, and what specific power they exercise, that is **how they mold the story.**

Example;

[1] Law and legal institutions are dominating life in this story;

[2] Churches shape individuals' values and norms;

[3] Politics influence public institutions' money spending.

(e) Investigate, what **groups** are involved in the story and try to formulate a **comparison** between your own peer group experiences and those other groups.

Example

Families are determined by the law that's beyond peer group experiences;

Peer groups are based on free emotions, families not;

Belonging is often more forceful and important than "official' group relations.

Ben

Now you have two leaflets with directives. Try to memorize them and be prepared to apply them once you [delete can] read the story that we offer you to analyze. It would be a great achievement, if you could bring the items of both leaflets together—you do not need to treat them in the order that is on the leaflets.

Mario

We invite Dave, Nick, Ritchie and Steve to enter this analysis game. You can do everything you used to do in your peer group. Try to work together, to discuss, to communicate, and if necessary to use your computer or other electronic devices. The goal of this exercise is not to obtain high grades (we don't grade this exercise) but to experience what's in the story and in the story telling. Stories do transfer other things than data alone, as you all know. They also express feelings, thoughts, perspectives, and emotions, they confront you with institutions in society, with forms of social life that are not always unproblematic to those involved in the story.

Ben

Now consider the following story. Its data and the main line of the narrative are also on your web site and you can—again—download those to your computer if you wish. Your comments can be given directly to us, and read into your devices. The text goes as the story has been told, and has not been edited.

The Story
(In Various Parts)

I

In Europe as well as in the US, legislators and Courts laid down rules for how their citizens must live together. In France, for instance, a rule was enforced in 1804 that man could not marry before having completed eighteen years, and woman before having completed fifteen years. Other Nations issued comparable rules and all decided on marriage as an extremely important form of life. In other words, all had an encompassing narrative on one of the central themes of living together. That narrative was, and still is, the one people should live in! No kidding, no questions. Boys and girls meet, at a certain age they are declared capable to live an adult life and to marry. That's the course of life.

Ben

OK, a first question. What is most evident in this story? It's often difficult to find answers to such questions.

What is evident, forms the basis of your behavior, and is not easy to perceive or to be subject of further investigation. Dave has asked "Didn't you tell us once that you could not see or study the fly in your eye?" Here we are again. You guess the answer. Evident in all rulings in all countries of the Western world is the gender difference. Boys are boys and girls are girls, and only they are allowed to marry! The traditional man-woman-kids family was the pillar of social life. Any presence of relatives did not change the picture. Ruling marriage is ruling sexual relations, ruling the division of goods and property as well as the application of a legally binding definition. Gender difference and age decide on the fundamentals of social life.

Mario

I remember a US television show, which started in the late eighties or the early nineties. It's called the Archie Bunker show. All vices and virtues of the traditional form of family life were demonstrated. I tell you more about that story.

During the many years that this show was on the air, some basics changed with the spirit of time. They referred to the nucleus of family life, the most important being gender difference. Archie and his wife first form a traditional family, even not purely a nucleus family but a rather extended group, including a daughter and her husband. Still no doubts about the genuine character of family.

Then, Archie meets his wife's lesbian cousin. Later he's confronted with divorce. The wife of Archie dies, his daughter separates from her husband and Archie becomes the custodian of a half-Jewish niece. How many potential family members are there in society? How strong is the nuclear family, who belongs and who does not belong? And why? How to define kinship, blood relations—what in fact are relatives? Do all in the family have to be treated equal? Who belongs to the family, who shares the goods and possessions, who profits from equality and membership? And who carries duties here? Is "the family" as defined by law given by nature? Rules which presumed "boys and girls" and laid down from let us say 1804, are highly debated today. New and pressing questions are posed to those who want to maintain the legal definitions of family, its rights and obligations included. The core issue is whether choices about living together really remain in tune with legal terms, regulations, and meanings.

Ben

These examples are not from inside families, but they pertain often to forces outside the family, like the administration, civil servants, politicians, and the like! They are at real distance to the cozy familial harmony!

I give you a next part of the story:

Look at the famous US Immigration and Naturalization Service, the INS, which treats a family unit only as those immediate members who reside together in the same household. That's a very, very restrictive interpretation of social reality today. Non-parental relatives outside the family home are excluded for the INS. If a family member is functionally part of another family, then these relatives are not allowed to immigrate with their parents. It's not a big jump from here to gay and lesbian persons who also are not allowed to embrace a form of marital belonging. Consider single parents stepfamilies, which also do not match the legal definitions enforced in society at large. What about the support of the 25% of US children living outside that INS definition? That's the essence of the first part of this story. As The American Home Economics Society stated around 1990, families sharing resources, responsibilities for persons and property, values and goals and who accepted various types of commitment over time, should be treated as such, regardless of blood, legal ties, adoption or marriage!

Ben

Now you've experienced how the concept of "family" is not a natural but rather an institutional fact. To define a "family" as such has its consequences! Legal and other social institutions maintain such a definition to also maintain the implicit order of norms and values, which go with that institution. A circular mechanism, indeed. But its applications are by no means circular or ineffective!

Mario

Let me add something more general. Each story has its moral understanding. The story teller aims at such morality, he or she shows what is hidden under the surface of appearances. He also aims at what has to be done, should be done because of that insight in underlying meanings. The subjects, the chains of causal events as well as the goals of the telling have to be clearly identified. It's up to you, for whom the story is told, to make decisions. And to apply its moral content! So all stories form an infinite chain. Also this one goes on. Read it:

You now understand the relevance of definitions of key concepts in social life. They include, and they exclude. Who is a member? A central question of belonging. Rather then solving the riddles of the story, it might be important to understand its moral implications. For yourself, for others, for friends and relatives, for students and teachers alike. I want to make it short. I tell you about a US legal case, known in American legal literature as the Sharon Kowalski case. Harvard Professor Martha Minow wrote extensively about this case, touching profound and challenging aspects.

One day, Sharon was hit by the car of a drunk driver, and left brain-damaged and disabled for life. Her middle-aged parents were loving and concerned parents, whose emotional life was anchored in conservative Christian values and had no other imagination about social relations then those rooted in the traditional definition of the family. As a consequence, they functioned also after

Sharon's catastrophe as parents in that sense of their understanding. Moreover, they acted upon the well-being of Sharon as if her role of being their daughter was the most natural one ever could conceive. The "best interest of the child" is a famous formula in family law on both sides of the Atlantic Ocean. It has an almost doctrinal function everywhere, an almost natural and super emotional value that needs no further comment. What parent does not act in the interest of its child? Shame on who dares to raise the question! So Sharon's parents took care of their daughter and acted in accordance with the given definition of family relations and in particular of responsible parenthood.

Dave

Let me say a word. Life is not as idyllic as you sketch out! My Dad once reminded me how there are many types of human relationships, gender relations and sexual preferences included. So, is this story not too simple? And why did it become a legal case? Is it in the law that we have to find the counterpart for the disturbed illusion of the idyll?

Mario

You have a good nose! The story was indeed too idyllic, and law plays a dominant role. Listen how it unfolds.

Steve

Well, is this not the happy end that every story in our society embraces, as you suggested before? Two interpretations—and the best was finally successful!

"Sharon appeared to have a very close friend, a lady whose name Karen Thompson became connected to Sharon's name. She visited the parents who were complete strangers to her, and desired to see Sharon. What appeared a disaster became disclosed in the course of that encounter. The parents had no knowledge about their daughter's sexual preferences nor about her plans and life expectations in the period before the accident. Their daughter Sharon had been living together with this Karen in a very warm and close lesbian relationship. They had bought and exchanged rings and were in the process of buying a house together. That house was at the point to become the home of both Sharon and Karen. Why would this not be realized now? The life of Sharon was not anchored in the concepts of family, marriage or house which were embraced by her parents. Why had her accident to bring her back to life patterns and values she had rejected before? She had not only rejected them, but had also come to a positive formation of other norms and values. She *had* a house of her own, and a *partner* that could take care of her! A house, a household, and a partner—were they not the necessary components of the traditional definition of a family in the sense of the law?

Apparently not. The parents were horrified and did not accept Karen's request to obtain guardianship of their daughter. That would have been the appropriate and legally valid way to bring Sharon to her home. The Court gave the parents guardianship, the Kowalskis barred Karen from visits to Sharon and tried to harm their relation[ship]. When in more recent years the parents became unfit to exercise that guardianship, they sought to appoint another person in their place, which the Court initially approved. Now, another Court has accepted Karen's request for guardianship, and in doing so recognized legal validity of relationships, which transcend the classical definition of a family."

Ben

That's a good analysis, and in the sense of what has been said about the structure of stories in general. However, Steve, you should underline again that things are less simple than they appear at face value. The story shows the dominance of our legal conceptualization of cornerstones of social life, such as marriage and family relationships. Peer groups are more or less free from that influence. Yet, as we concluded several times before, peers are comparable to other social institutions such as family life, especially when you look at the structures they share.

Mario

I would add that there is a problem of loyalty and commitment, also going to the heart of peer experiences. Do you leave a peer friend with the snap of a finger? You don't. Would you not go to Court (if you were old enough for litigation) to help a friend? You would. Is there never a deep conflict of loyalties in your group? There surely is. Like here. The parents are loyal to their child, like Karen is loyal to Sharon. There is no objective evaluation of both loyalties, and both commitments seem genuine. However, they are genuine within different sets of value orientations. The law sustains one, not the other. Changes of public opinion after years of suffering cause the law to choose that other option. Thanks God, some say. Others still proclaim how the law is becoming another nihilistic social enterprise! You got it?

Ben

Let me finish this story you guys have to analyze. One issue was not yet mentioned, although it is important.

"The parents' obligation to act in the best interest of their child includes their recognition of the fact that they don't have the right to autonomously define that interest. Any adult child has the right to choose an appropriate life form. They in fact did not respect their child's choices, in particular her choice to define for herself what the definition of family should be for her. She already had chosen before the accident. After being informed, the Kowalskis were challenged to respect that choice! That is beyond doubt a difficult task for parents. It is, however, an essential issue in the life of human beings."

Ben

Now, Steve, Dave, Nick, Ritchie and girls—take your time, your energy and your intelligence to come to your analysis of this story. Take the two leaflets and use them as a guideline. Use your computer either for info or for writing down your observations. Discuss as much as you like, and let your results honor your peer group! What a challenge!

Scene 2:
"Inclusion, Exclusion"

Images and Sounds

A few days later, the friends are with the teachers in the same classroom. They are heading for another session in the Peer Groups Program.

Ben

Here we are again. Our subject might change, but not our method. Today I'll try to make it short. Last time it took many hours. Your considerations of the story were not easy, and its consequences were quite a burden to some of you, who never had thought about such things. For any one of us, reconsidering what happened in our earliest days is difficult. Not only adolescents, but also many adults, don't take the trouble to do just that. Others leave it to a shrink to help them function.

Mario

Ben, let us come back to the first leaflet we've handed out. I guess that the first and most general part of those observations is acceptable and has been understood well. The questions of the second section are more difficult. They remain an important subject of discussion. I observed a certain consensus about the first question of that section among the boys, less so among the girls. However, peer groups seem neither autonomous nor supplementary for boys and girls. A common feature to boys and girls is that they fulfil a supplementary role by means of emphasizing their autonomy. Is that correct? Please consult your notes on the issue! What do you think that the ideas of your parents about this issue would be?

Steve

I find in all my notes an approval of that idea. Our parents would be nearer to our experiences if they would join that consideration! A peer group can indeed be supplementary to norms and forms of life in school or family—but only if its autonomy is accepted. That's a difficult issue for many! Moreover, there is no genuinely bad influence of peer groups on individual members. What is called a bad influence is mostly a different or adversary attitude relative to the family's standard values. To define 'bad' and 'good' is difficult in this context! The exceptions are violence, theft or other behaviors. Gangs more frequently initiate that behavior than peer groups ever would.

I wrote sort of an essay about these and other experiences, my feelings and opinions. Mario told me to bring the text with me so that you can download and discuss it. Quite a burden, but I like it.

Mario

So listen to and read Steve's story, and consult for a second time the leaflet about "Story Analysis". Find the forms of belonging, and their degrees of intensity. Detect the major decision-making opinions, attitudes, and motivations as well as their corresponding institutions. Not too difficult, I hope? Steve's essay on "The World of Peers" goes as follows:

Steve's Essay

"The world of peers is a world of friends, the world of a modern North American tribe. I don't know whether this tribe exists in other parts of the Western world. It's remarkable how this world seems adult-free, as if it took its model from the world of video games or Internet chat corners. I don't know whether that is entirely true. You don't find many adults, that's for sure. But one experiences their presence in all corners of that world. A virtual presence, a normative presence. Pressures all around. Adults create the norms that we contest; adults determine the policies we live by, and adults contest or approve adolescent behaviors. They make the difference! In fact, they do that all the time and everywhere. To make differences seems the most important job to fulfil.

Those differences stem from the social mechanisms of inclusion and exclusion. Anthropologists discovered how 'defining the family' is one of those essential mechanisms in all of human cultures. The same scheme is applied to groups in general. It is simple, and tells us to lay formally down who does, and who does not belong to the group! Laws are issued about what type of marriage is allowed, and what type of marriage is forbidden. Of course, there are rights to oppose a proposed marriage, but the most powerful decision is not in opposing a marriage—it is on defining a man or a woman as an individual that is allowed to freely marry all other individuals with the exception of…It's the exception to the rule that counts! In direct lineage, marriage is in almost all Western countries prohibited by law between all ascendants and legitimate or illegitimate descendents and relatives by marriage in the same lineage. In collateral lineage, marriage is prohibited between legitimate or illegitimate brother and sister. finally, It's prohibited to marry between uncle and niece, aunt and nephew. That's what I found in the official papers! Sounds great, doesn't it? It seems a nearly unlimited freedom.

Look at the distinctions made to construct a difference. To tell someone that he or she is not allowed to marry his or her aunt or uncle means to oblige him or her to marry only those who are neither aunt nor uncle. Nobody ever defined who is aunt or uncle. Their definition depends on the culture we live in. The same is true for the more abstract idea of lineage, not to mention the hypermodern concept of genealogical tree that plays such an important role in our hospitals when cases of genetic research and consult are at stake. Could I conclude in general, that all prohibitions are an order? I guess, I could!"

Mario

Steve furthermore explains what he was thinking about peer groups, where mechanisms of inclusion and exclusion are also at work.

Steve's Essay 2

"Let me be clear about all prohibitions. Laws, rules, and prohibitions issued by school boards, administrators, lawmakers, civil servants, teachers, and parents do consequently not only say what you should not do, but in saying so they rather (often in the first place) mean to say what you must do! This mechanism is a great force in peer group life. If our peers result from the difference we make between others and ourselves (who do not belong), than we find in our belonging the force of following the rules we make! Somebody wrote about peer influences on individuals 'You are whom you hang around with'. Yeah, that's very much it! Because hanging around means being in order! The riddle of peer groups—it does not disturb you to be defined pretty much by your friends. It provides you a backbone no family ever could. For that, you do not need to have many things in common, like adults suggest. Adults defend their friendships and cute little groups by what they say they have in common. We don't <u>have</u> much in common—we <u>are</u> common. We look at ourselves not the way our parents and teachers look at us, we have our friends as the mirror that shows us who and how we are.

You feel it, friends? If you do, you understand more than my parents ever did! They think there is only one sort of friendship, one based on mutual respect or even love, based on sharing, on common interests, on common views, attitudes, motivations. Our peer group provides an order when we hang around, no matter for how long or what we share or do not share! It's the difference that makes the order. Difference? Don't you think that we, adolescents, make our own differences when we fight for being in the group? Fight, yes. We have to, and create the vital difference, manage the dynamics of inclusion and exclusion! Climb over the wall: of course, we did not invent this power; our parents' ethics was the first hint of it. Their attitude is 'to give their kids the greatest autonomy possible'; they 'don't get in their kids' faces'! You remember how every prohibition is also a command? 'Not to get in the kids' face' has the effect of 'leave them under all circumstances'. Not we left home, family, parents and found peers, but they left us! Is that all we need?

We became a peer-driven generation because of that superior difference which is based on the ultimate command to leave us alone! Indeed, we spend a lot of time alone. More than our parents could ever think of in their youth. And don't forget how our peer groups are not durable. Their time-span might be a weekend, a holiday, or a school semester. Your best friends are only a few! Belonging is crucial for that reason."

Mario

Steve has already referred to the comparison with family life and with marriage as one of its core issues. A difference is made—often in the form of a prohibition that works as a command. He suggests that the prohibition not to get in your kids' face has worked as a command to leave them. Hence their need for peer groups, no matter whether they are durable or not.

Steve's Essay 3

"There is one more idea to comment on. It's in the well-known proverb that you do not and cannot choose your relatives, but you do choose your friends! That's an important distinction again, one that also pertains to inclusion and exclusion. As if you are fully responsible for the friends you have, not for the family you're in. In other words, the latter are a matter of fate and the former of rational decision. Is that correct? How does this idea fit into the fact that all civil relations are legally determined? We do not feel the legal difference between family relations and those of friendship, but they are huge if it comes to a situation of conflict. Parents and kids cannot give testimony in court; they have a specific stand there. Law treats blood relations differently from all other relations.(in limited ways). Law creates differences, which create loyalties, fidelities. your feelings or emotions don't count, but the degrees of kinship or consanguinity do. Those degrees are laid down in laws and court decisions.

These are treated like other legal concepts, such as contract, offense, property, or loan. What counts is the meaning in law that has been given to them. The discourse of law first determines how x is y, and then follows the prescription that one has to live as if all y is real, and forget about x! No wonder that actual deliberations are on the balance between a broad and a strict understanding of the meaning of 'family'. 'What is y?' is the question! Is marriage a form of friendship? No, it's a y; it's a contract. Is a peer group a form of friendship? Yes, because it's not a y—feel free to call it a x! I am not absolutely sure, but I would guess that the relations between peer groups and school classes would become treated in the very same way! Classes are like family—they are not chosen, at least not by the students, to whom They are a form of fate. And classes are institutionally made. Hence the class is legally relevant. The class defines you; you do not define the class. The existence of peer groups in class is a riddle. They exist under the surface of class schemes, class plans, class groups, and class rosters. Yet, they make a difference!

Rachel

What a text. Lots of ideas and knowledge in its few lines! Have to think about it, and to discuss. It's not a girl's text. We would have a different emphasis!

Mario

Sure, we need your feedback! Do not forget to consult the "story analysis" notes for your understanding of that text. How clear is it that forms of belonging or distances in patterns of social relationships are at stake, and institutions are at work in the text. How does law mold some issues of the story? You can give a really clear answer this time! It might be more difficult to decide upon opinions, attitudes, and motivations. Yet it must be evident for you how they play a predominant role. I wish you luck; go ahead! See you next time; I'll read you on the web site or when you mail me your notes. In any case, we'll discuss your observations next time we meet.

Ben

Let me add: It might be difficult for you to determine the structure of the story. Who's the real subject? The peer group, the adolescent individual, the parent? Or perhaps society at large? Then follows a next question. Where's the chain of causalities? Is it the parent's ethics, or perhaps the violent society and its requirement to construct 'shadow families' or maybe other substitutes? Or is the law the creator of causal events, saying that after the first concept comes the next, and then the next, and so on…? And if this chain is finite, what then is the moral issue at stake in this story? Are individuals good and peers bad, or are peers bad but individuals good? Is law and order mirrored in peers like in gangs or *mafiosi*? Are peers better educators than parents, school, and social institutions together? Many possibilities to consider, many questions not to hide from…Good Luck!

Steve

I do not trust my ears. I cannot believe this! Where am I? In your computers, or on the Net?

Ben

What?

Steve

Your questions would lead to disclosing the structure of my narrative. I lose control.

Rachel

I guess I understand his feelings. He's the author, it seems you forgot that!

Ben

Why?

Steve

You know, I've written this text as an honest attempt to come to terms with everything that has been said until now about peer groups and families. That touched me, you know. It touches fundamentals of your opinion and your feelings of security. Those considerations are also mine. They are written, but they remain mine, uniquely mine. Now you come and challenge all of us to unravel the structure of my narrative. As if I did not write the text, but functioned as the servant of an unknown force that ordered me to write such and so…This really unnerves me! Are we the servant of the story-structure when we tell a story our way?

Mario

I think I understand. Does he exist, this absolutely unique storyteller? All meanings, all language must be a common good and offered along commonly accepted lines. If you do not accept these norms, you're lost. Nobody can ever understand you! Words and meanings of words are the property of all of us. If not, we would be lost! That's basic, you know! Very basic indeed.

Scene 3:
"One and Many"

Images and Sounds

The six students meet with their teachers for the third and last time. They are in the same classroom. It is clear from their faces that they'd like to enter the Program again, but are also glad to finish, to wrap it up and look ahead for another Program to live with, like they did with the Peer Program. Yet, they still have to complete the Peer Groups session in order to exit. This is an early morning session. Mario and Ben appear to be in a good mood.

Mario

Good Morning! We're not doing a text analysis again, although that's a great technique. We will offer you only fragments of texts, which are accompanied by short and clear questions. The situations as described in those texts differ in opinion, attitude, and experience from yours, I am sure. However, Mario and I thought they were just the right phrases to confront you with on a variety of issues, which other adolescents who do not share your daily life, have to face.

Ben

Peer groups are normally limited to friends that belong to the same social structure in society. They are not racially mixed or with important differences in level of income or life style. And they are certainly not uniting boys and girls! Yet, all peer members share concerns about life and struggle to keep their own position in modern society like all of you do!

Mario

Let me try to explain this last part. We want you to take the questions that are presented here as titles of a paragraph, as if they were your own concerns. Their answers and considerations will surely differ from yours, and that's exactly what interests us most. Give us your comment on the answers, and tell us in a separate column your feelings about the confrontation. Here are the texts and their titles that formulate the essential questions. Limit your interaction until you've been through all of them.

1. "WHAT IT TAKES TO BE ACCEPTED".
GIRLS' PEER GROUPS:

"Popularity is such an interesting issue in seventh grade. The kids are really aware of what it takes to fit in, and what it takes now is pretty hard to achieve. Whether you think clothes are important sort of places you in a group. If you think clothes are important and you like being well dressed, or you like dressing a way that could put you in a group. Our group sort of has their own kind of fashion. We shop about six different stores and we all kind of keep up with the trends. The makeup thing sort of puts you in a group, too. Our group tends to wear a lot more makeup than other people do. I want to look not generally older but just nice-looking."

"There is a clique of popular people, and everybody else is not included. It's like they don't really care about anybody else but themselves. You have to be the same supermodel that everybody else is. Two pounds and a Gap lover with the same hair, same haircut. Same straight looks. They all look the same if you ask me. It's just one big chain of followers. The people in the popular group say there is no peer pressure—because they are at the top of the food chain."

"The popular clique usually knows exactly what's in. People make fun of you or talk behind your back. And there is actually a lot of talking behind people's backs. Sometimes it's not so bad; it's just like funny stories. But sometimes it's like making fun of someone's outfit or 'Did you hear what they did today?'"

Maria

What a wonderful text! I feel exactly the same, and think this must be the case for Rachel also. A very good description of our situation now, and our views on the immediate future, sort of map for what is ahead! I must say, I hate the Gap lover and avoid the populars. But sometimes you have to join, or to accept such behavior. Is that pressure? I don't know. It's the way of life; even at our age where we feel free, we are obliged.

Ben

Glad to hear that. OK, now the text for the boys. You are older now, but what is your reaction?

Boys' Peer Groups:

"Spring break rules at 13! At this point, I'd rather go on vacation with my friends than with my family. You have no limits, no boundaries; you just do what you want, get as tan as you want, party as long as you want. People that don't go on spring break, they just sit at home and watch TV and just go to the tanning booth so it looks like they've been somewhere."

2. "MONICA AND ADAM"
—She and me; He and me?—"

"Monica and I have been going out for four months, three days. 'Going out' at thirteen isn't just like the cootie stuff or just like seeing them and saying 'Hi'. It's sort of serious. You're not shy. You actually do stuff with them. You even talk to them—even if it's just over the phone."

"Having a boyfriend is OK when you're thirteen and it's considered a normal thing. Adam, my boyfriend, was angry last night because some guys had said that they likes me, and he got really jealous of that, and some girls were saying that I was flirting back with them. And then Adam got mad at those girls because he thought that they were trying to break Adam and I up. Then one of his friends came up to me to tell me that he wanted to talk to me just to make sure I wasn't mad at Adam. But I thought that he was coming to tell me that Adam was going to dump me! So I just liked to walk away from him, and the Adam thought I was mad at him. And then we finally got together and were dancing, and he just said he was never going to dump me and that he never thought of that, and that it was great going out with me, and I like agreed. And everything was great then.

3. "My fears and worries, like everyone's of my age".

"Thirteen is a hard age, very hard. A lot of people say you have it easy, you're a kid, but there's a lot of pressure being 13—to be respected by people in your school, to be liked, always feeling like you have to be good. There's pressure to do drugs, too, so you try not to succumb to that. But you don't want to be made fun of, so you have to look cool. You wear the right shoes, the right clothes—then it's all right."

"There are a lot of transitions going on, a lot of moving around. It's not like you know what's going to happen tomorrow. Life gets different when you get older—there's more work. And when you go to college it's hard because you're alone for the first time. But when you get out of college you start to establish yourself and who you think you are and what you're about. That's a good time".

Nick

This is particularly true. I remember having exactly those feelings. To establish yourself is, however, not for some months or even a year. It seems sort of a process, never ending and always demanding! I never regretted my efforts to enter my group.

Ben

Well, let's finish with an exceptional idea. Can you be a peer group on your own, or is that impossible because on your own, you're not a group? Consider the following situation:

"I'm thirteen. I went to Toy Toys with my products and they treated me with, like, respect. They set me up as a vendor. It was great. I got my first order and money. I think I get the money off my sales. I'm doing pretty well. I'm putting all the money I make in investments. Until I'm 35. My mom said to me, 'I'm going to invest your money,' and I was, like, 'OK'. My friends think it's pretty cool, but we don't really talk about it. I'd like to try the drive-through at McDonald's. I just think it would be fun, working there".

Dave

Yeah; it's pretty cool indeed. Have to think about it, like we all do—the girls included, I guess! You'll hear from us, Ben, Mario. Within a week, look at our web sites!

§ 5 Teachers' Feedback

"The best of adolescence was the intense male friendships—not
only because of the cozy feelings of camaraderie they afforded boys
coming unstuck from their close-knit families, but because
of the opportunity they provided for uncensored talk...for my part
I associate that amalgam of mimicry, reporting, kibbitzing, disputation, satire,
and legendizing...like the folk narrative of a tribe passing from one
stage of human development to the next. Also, those millions
of words were the means by which we either took vengeance on or tried to hold
at bay the cultural forces that were shaping us. Instead of stealing cars
from strangers, we sat in the cars we had borrowed from our fathers
and said the wildest things imaginable, at least in our neighborhood.
Which is where we were parked.

Philip Roth: *Writing and the Powers That Be*, 1974

1. Introduction

Teachers encounter an interactive and e-educational program that promotes
the enhancement of responsive citizenship and helps adolescents to understand and to manage their "Peer Groups"—not through psychotherapy or
authoritarian guidance, but by means of interactive exploration of its major
dimensions.

It has been emphasized in the discussions how several fundamental issues
are important, such as:

Adolescents are "contemplators"; they think about future changes in their life in terms of commitments, in particular those to their "peer groups", and need skilful consideration of their motivations and future behaviors.

Adolescents experience their commitments as exclusively private, despite the fact that these are dominated by institutions such as schools, life styles, civil life, and family.

Adolescents have difficulty in understanding how their commitments to peer groups are forms of judgment and evaluations rather than indicators for an objective state of affairs. Explorations of this nature lead to responsive citizenship and an increased quality of life that goes with diminished social costs.

This "Peers" program is conceived for ages 13–16. However, the program is an emotionally and intellectually enriching experience to younger teens as well as to adults. Different coaching is required in all those cases. Indications pertaining to 'teachers training' lay the groundwork for their important advisory service. The training should convey the major background ideas and perspectives of the programs that are used in a variety of contexts. All training activity is important at all age levels and all institutions should have access, since focus is on the major semantics of institutions in modern society. The latter dominate the forms and practices of communication. Understanding institutions and acting in accordance with their normative patterns, values, and expectations has often been regarded as a by-product of cognition, and not as a subject of education in its own right.

This training leads to a very different perspective. Cognition appears to be embedded in institutions—not institutions in cognition! Students consequently have to understand the peculiarities of institutional life and its specific features, which dominate their emotions, feelings, and experiences, and leave a mark on their acquired cognition.

2. The Program as a Narrative

A first concern when confronted with this "Peers" program is to understand how it offers a narrative, a dialogue, and displays its interactive character. A fundamental achievement is therefore the full mastering of the narrative plot. The following questions can assist teachers to come to such understanding.

1.Analyze and reconstruct the narrative as "The Story of Peers".
In doing so, consider the following aspects:
(a) How does the narrative unfold?
(b) Grasp its dynamics.
(c) How are the various persons in the story introduced?
(d) Describe their perspectives on life as they become involved in the course of events, and consider
(e) What effect the latter have on the outcome of the story.

2. The following exercises introduce to the full meaning of the narrative:
(a) Try to give a profile of the different characters that are involved,
(b) Describe and discuss their functions and
(c) Show their limitations as caused by the various roles they have to fulfil.
Those exercises can be accomplished through answering the following, more difficult questions:
(d) How would you bring those different character patterns together into one, all embracing picture, and
(e) Could you elaborate on the interrelations of all these characters?
(f) Since each of these characters has a specific task and interest within the totality of the narration, and since [delete also] the narration [also] has a task and interest within the education of the student, how would you evaluate this task and interest in your own words?

(g) Could you enter your classroom and narrate to the students the "Peers" narrative and the aspect[s] (a) to (f) as if it was a coherent story and you were its storyteller?

(f) How would you in that case include the specific stories, especially those told in Part III? What place and function do they have in the program, how do they differ from the unfolding story of Part I and Part II. Could you agree, and explain, that Part II is a "meta-story" in relation to Part I? What type of "meta-story" is offered here, why is that the case, and can you defend the idea that this is a consequence of the interactive character of the Programs?

3. The Education Process

The following points can inspire one to find more issues to consider:

1). First and very important points of attention are:

a) The selection of the main issues in the "Peers" narration,

b) To find their place in the context of events and

c) To acquire insight in the narration's internal order that eventually leads to the student's internalization of the major concepts and meanings.

2). The contrast between the design of the "Peers" program and the general features of curriculum education should be a subject of consideration. To begin with, consider questions like:

a) Where would you place the major issues in the "Peers" narration in the context of regular curriculum programs?

b) Could you determine their position in those regular programs?

c) Could you design a comparison with the "Peers" program you study now?

d) How would you evaluate the two types of positions and contexts?

3). In order to assist you when formulating an answer to the question 2d, pay attention to the following issues:

a) The differences between regular curriculum education and the interactive and dialogue-based approach should become clear in the manner the subjects [delete at hand] are treated, as well as their literal formulation. Examples of that different approach are all over the "Peers" texts.

b) The latter embrace emotion, experience, and narration as equivalent elements of an encompassing method and form a contrast to the analytical and individualistic approach of curriculum education.

c) The social context of all events and actions, as constructed by the narration, forms a contrast to many curriculum textbooks. There are major differences, which relate to the theoretical explanations in the preceding chapters of this book. Those differences may have an important meaning for all students.

4) The introduction of the "Peers" program as an education device that can eventually be used in regular settings will require a firm opinion pertaining to at least three important aspects of the program. Mastering that opinion may result in a positive effect of all training.

a) Observe the dialogue-based elements in the "peers" program. Consider how they contribute to enhance the profit from that approach when combining the latter with regular curriculum elements.

b) What electronic devices (walkie-talkie, computer keyboards and mats, cellular phones, computers, electronic notebooks and the like) enhance those dialogue-based aspects in class or groups outside classes? Is there a contradiction or a tension between the use of electronic devices and the dialogue-based education, or are they complementary?

c) The "Peers" program enables to explicitly practice forms of co-assessment in class. Consider that method in general. Would you be able to introduce that co-assessment also in other education programs? Describe your own role and position during the process of co-assessment in class.

4. Education Goals

This program is designed to be entertaining, instructive and dialogue-based interactive to the students. To understand the construction of this text implies a thorough understanding of communication in the age of electronics:

* Students have the possibility to answer the voices that speak to them, and reflect their inner dialogues at the same time. The teacher(s) are in dialogue with the student and his or her classmates, as teachers are involved in dialogues in the program texts. The students ask and are asked questions, and their answers should be saved electronically so that they can be confronted with their earlier opinions.

* Images of natural scenes, of animals, landscapes, airplanes, maps, texts, diagrams, city pavements, sidewalk cafés that accompany the conversation(s) are shown by computer images intermittently, sometimes quickly, sometimes slowly and with precision. Where the student has to answer questions, or to write words or sentences, the program and its images and sounds must give sufficient opportunity to perform that task. Again, the spoken answers or written texts should always remain electronically available for later showing and/or revision. Sounds of narrator voices, of animals, of music, of traffic noises, or just of the wind, should be integrated in the program in such a manner that there is sufficient variation of loudness, and concentration supported by pictures as well as sounds.

* The openness of the program should in particular be realized where a dialogue between the characters in the program leaves a place for the students to enter whenever they like to do so. For each student, all elements of dialogue should be saved for later feedback!

* The goals are manifold. The program is designed to train students in appropriately understanding underlying patterns of "evident" situations in everyday life. Such an understanding is of utmost importance to the quality of the decisions they make in later life, in particular as citizens in our future society. When judging that quality, focus is on responsibility of individuals, and (individual) responsibility is the major point of reference for decision-making. The ability to be accountable is not the outcome of natural growth but of training and education in general.

It must be made clear from the beginning that each fragment of daily life gives access to the underlying patterns of reality, from toasting a bagel for breakfast to taking a swim, from acquiring a position in the peer group to riding a bike. That access must be learned, and it does not come without effort and purposeful training.

The "Peer Groups" text challenges the student to place him or herself in a network of intimate as well as public relationships, so that the understanding of those networks contributes to the student's identity formation.

"Peer Groups" shows in particular the strong grip of social institutions and their legal patterns on the multiple meanings inherent in the everyday reality. This type of knowledge and understanding is lacking in many standard education curriculums. This educational method emphasizes the importance of understanding the institutional patterning of social relations and the structure of society in which students must develop their identity.

The "Peer Groups" program challenges the student's intelligence to understand and manage complex meanings and relations where at a first glance there is nothing to be seen or observed. One of the basic experiences will be that, where no apparent conflict or interest is at stake, there is still an important reservoir of meaning in facts and events at work. The discovery of that reservoir, as well as its exploitation, requires training. The program includes the use of electronic devices. They enrich the experience of the students, train them during the exercises in the use of computers etc., and enhance the opportunity of communicating with other students, both real and virtual. The world of the student's images can be directed and stimulated through the use of computer-related programs, and the program also provides numerous possibilities for feedback on discussions, information, and the like. Furthermore, computer use facilitates the consultation or coordination of other programs, which sustain individual decisions to be made during the accomplishment of this program.

5. Education Issues

The following issues in the diverse scenes are specifically in-built educational clusters of importance:

Part I, Scene 1.

* Entering specific social groups is often a matter of deliberate decision-making and not a matter of natural behavior.

* Peer groups are everywhere in adolescent as well as adult life. Their existence is not specific for the contemporary teen life style.

* Moral pressures are a considerable concern to adolescents. Those pressures represent the adult world in sometimes oppressive manners.

Part I, Scene 2.

* Parallels between family life and peer groups are important.

* The self-fulfillment of adolescents in peer groups depends on the family's attitude towards such groups. A positive opinion of parents and other family members can sustain the identity formation of teens in their groups.

* The many forms of family life, beyond the two parents-kids form of life, are all relevant to peer group experiences.

Part II, Scene 1.

* The structure of a story, of any story, determines thought patterns and patterns of action even in adolescent peer groups.
* The structure of stories relates to all types of social institutions.

Part II, Scene 2.

* Features of educational institutions in comparison with peer group life are an important issue in the experiences of teens.
*Peer experiences and social life are explained in terms of "peers as a speech community"—an important paradigm that relates to theoretical explanations in the preceding chapters of this book.

Part II, Scene 3.

*Observations and basic questions pertaining to peer groups are summarized on the blackboard.

Part III, Scene 1.

* The performance of story-analysis.

Part III, Scene 2.

*Sharon's story and Steve's text as an object for analysis.

Part III, Scene 3.

* Texts on various themes in peer group experience, mainly from the perspective of 13-year-old teens.

A Final Note

This list of educational issues justifies and exemplifies not only the introduction of the "Peer Groups" texts, but also reinforces the theoretical paragraphs of the book with the narratives that approximate real-life situations. Also in this chapter, communication and semantics of communication are the major issue at stake.

CHAPTER V

SOCIAL DIMENSIONS OF E-EDUCATION

§ 1. Introduction

§ 2. Human Plasticity

Change and Plasticity
Artifices Shape Communication
Philosophical Anthropology
Psychology
Lifespan Psychology and the Sociology of the Course of Life

§ 3. Neurology, Brain Research, E-communication And E-education

PET-scan Locations
The Mouse at Three
Brains and Computers
The Range of our Capabilities
The Brain and the Skull: Inside and Outside
Plasticity Again

§ 4. The Connected Citizens

§ 1. Introduction

Does E-communication exist because of the sophisticated machinery we allow to enter into one of our most human properties, which is communication? Yes, it does. Is Aristotle's understanding of the human being as a "social animal" enhanced by the introduction of electronic artifices? Yes, it is the case. But what is the meaning of this latter observation, and what meaning has it specifically in view of education, being one of the root processes of becoming human?

Many answers were given in the previous chapters[xxxii]. Education in general and E-education in particular have the "E•-" artifice in full operation in all dimensions of communication. The "E•-" stands, as was often emphasized, not only for "*e*lectronic", but also for "*e*nhancement", "*e*xperience," or "a new *e*xcellence". They are altogether new ornaments of our daily communication in educational settings and all result from *e*lectronics, which could be considered as the breeding ground for artifices in our modern life.

E-communication finds us in a situation that resembles modern medicine in many ways. We are in both cases astonished and fascinated, frightened and questioning, when we perceive and experience how artifices do change the many properties of body and mind, which we naïvely call "ours". We hardly know how to master those new techniques and their meanings in ordinary life, so that the expression "ours" seems to have become perverted or alienated. As a consequence, our descriptions of what happens or what has happened flounder, and our metaphors become inadequate. The world of our artifices in daily and immediate experiences is more disassociated than ever and C.P.Snow's traditional thesis about our "living in two cultures" appears hopelessly antiquated.

§ 2. Human Plasticity

So it seems that there is more to do then just filling a gap, and more to consider than just the intrusion of the artificial in the realm of our authentically human communication. The concept of *change* is perhaps the only one that articulates the essence of these new communicative processes. But how should we understand *change*? What is change and on what is change based?

Indeed, to educate is to change, and education is a continued participation in processes of change. Teacher and student have to fulfill their roles in this change on an equal footing. Our preceding chapters underlined how *interactivity* is the state of mind in which this equality is realized. Education necessarily enhances interactivity. It was described how each teacher changes the student and through this he himself changes—not just once, but continuously.

Change and Plasticity

Heraclites colors our insight. We remember him saying that 'it is not possible to step into the same river twice', and he thus suggested that we therefore never exit the same stream we entered. In this light, we never ever meet the same person twice! To communicate and to educate is a lifetime work in progress—a progress that focuses on the *work itself* rather than any fixed goals that make progress instrumental.

But how do we situate the change of student and teacher in—and during their communication? That question is of general nature and so is its answer. The two lead unmistakably to the foundations of change as a general feature of the human condition. An important foundational insight is that all *plasticity* of mind and life manifests itself as *change*. We are, however, not used to honor and accept that plasticity as an omnipresent and ever challenging force in life. If plasticity is favorable, we often accept it joyfully and fully exploit the plasticity—but if it does not appear to be of any use, we feel threatened by that force, and tend to neglect or deny it.

This interplay of denial and acceptance shapes communication and education in particular. For instance, we judge a person as "having no backbone" when he changes his position continuously with the argument that he honors his plasticity in doing so. If he eats things he and we never eat under normal circumstances, but does so in order not to starve, we agree; we accept and perhaps even admire his manifest plasticity. But if he defends a viewpoint that we deem asocial and stupid on that same ground, we do not. Plasticity—yes, we know about it! But plasticity is apparently not the foundation of our self-understanding and our basic patterns of knowledge!

Artifices Shape Communication

How come? Why do we make *plasticity* a normative issue? That's the fundamental question about artifices shaping our communication. Plasticity and its inherent 'change' are keys to our self-understanding. They are also keys to understand the image that represents our self and mirrors that self in the multiplicity of social relations in all cultural regards—education included. This has normative consequences: does the teacher not dare to present himself or herself to the students as a human being gifted with plasticity and transferring that plasticity to them? Where is the teacher who primarily presents himself as a being-in-plasticity? Only E-communication sheds a light on such positions in social life and highlights aspects we never perceived before.

That leads instantly to a reconsideration of some important points of interest, which were discussed in the preceding chapters. The first point is the fact that the concept of *human plasticity* is a fundamental insight in human nature.

The idea that *'to communicate'* always means *'to change'* appears inherent in that consideration. Moreover, one must conclude that there is consequently no *citizenship* possible without e-communicative skills and practices in modern society.

Plasticity is a source for all communications between humans. Faces change when they talk, or when people are addressed, and people are on the move when they become part of an ongoing narration. Plasticity is the mother of expressiveness, and there is no experience in a human life without a functioning plasticity. But it is difficult to understand plasticity as a concept. It has many names and depends on contexts of a different nature. Three of those contexts are important to focus on; together they constitute a century-long conceptualization of human plasticity. A first is in philosophy and a second in psychology—both evolved in the past century—and a third marks the beginning of the new century with studies in neurology, with brain research as well as cell biology.

Philosophical Anthropology

Philosophical anthropology flourished in Germany in the 1920s, together with philosophy of life *(Lebensphilosophie)*, existentialism, and phenomenology. It later became important after the Second World War and still later in France, Spain, Italy, Belgium, and The Netherlands. That complex branch of thought developed philosophical considerations on what sciences had discovered about the nature of man and the human condition in general. It is clear that the scientific discoveries of that time were very different from the present, but the approach was fruitful and sufficiently general to be effective today. The concept of plasticity is of core interest in this context.

Max Scheler, Helmuth Plessner, Arnold Gehlen, and Adolph are still honored as influential in European philosophy. Their contributions reached far beyond the boundaries of the German language. This is thanks to (a) their contribution to the emerging social sciences, in particular sociological theory, and (b) to their strong influence on French phenomenology.

Authors such as Merleau-Ponty or Jean Paul Sartre relate intimately to the project of a philosophical anthropology. They tried to adapt phenomenology to a philosophy of consciousness, having the original descriptions of Husserl and his theory of intentionality in mind. Consciousness is always directed at objects, Husserl's theory said. However, the question arose whether such directedness is only possible through special mental entities called 'meanings', or whether we need another concept of consciousness for solving such questions. Merleau-Ponty questioned the power of phenomenological descriptions to reveal human consciousnesses. He stressed the role of the active, involved body in all human knowledge. So he thus foreshadowed our recent theories of mental processes and their biological basis, as well as the dogma of dividing matter from mind.

Phenomenology had a pervasive influence in theology, sociology, psychology, psychiatry, and literary criticism, and became, in the perspective of general culture, one of the mainstreams in modern philosophy. That importance was already implied in the project of a philosophical anthropology. Phenomenological reiterations of that project have in the US become widely known through "symbolic interactionism", including philosophers such as Mead, Parsons or Schutz. The 'symbolic' represents the artifice in all domains of interaction.

One example pertains directly to the concept of 'plasticity'. It is based on the play on words one finds in Plessners foundational publications[xxxiii]. The Latin expression 'natura' plays a dominant role in philosophy. The question is whether a human being, its body and mind and operational activity, are a phenomenon of *nature*, of (as philosophers in the Middle Ages conceived) a *natura naturans* (a 'pure nature', one would say in the language of everyday)? All facts of culture speak against that viewpoint, and yet it is difficult to conceive the specificity of an independent human nature.

The long-lived contrast between nature and culture seems to have never been solved. There is no culture where pure nature reigns. Human culture exists in all its histories and variant forms thanks to the non-natural, the artifice. But that artifice is so deeply rooted in human self-consciousness that it is hard to have a grip on the distinction between one and the other. Plessner played with the words 'artificial' and 'natural', stating that a human life unfolds in the sphere of a 'natürliche Künstlichkeit', which is translatable as 'natural artificiality'.

One can also invert the order of words and form another expression, which then reads 'künstliche Natürlichkeit': an artificial naturalness. In the first expression, the artifice becomes so natural, that neither the human body nor the human mind is ever aware anymore about the distance it has bridged to nature. But is it then still possible to properly determine the role and function of the natural? It seems, that the *natural* itself is an expression of *artificial* origin—and that dimension is in the second expression.

When speaking of nature, Plessner would say: one acts *artificially*. Using the word 'nature' is in itself an act of non-natural (or artificial) character, and the expression only works well if one accepts the intertwining of the natural and the artificial into one meaningful expression. To maintain the distinction between the two components as if they were distinguishable entities disturbs a truly *human* world-view. The openness of the human mind towards its own history and the multiple forms of life in a diversity of cultures rests upon the specific artificiality of the human nature.

Humans seem to live, Plessner and others suggest, in a world that is man's *second nature*—intertwining the artificial and the natural such that the artificial is as natural as the natural is artificial. The ability to intertwine is exactly what the concept "plasticity" lays out. And E-communication is yet another form of such intertwining, one should conclude from those studies in philosophical anthropology.

Psychology

The thought patterns and articulations of a philosophical anthropology have not lost any meaning or value in later years, although their context has changed considerably. They have been overridden by more specific scientific discoveries about the human mind, its material basis and its dimensions of action and patterning.

Emphasis on *the psychology of social dimensions* is evident when the development of human beings has become a subject of study beyond philosophy. The fundamental question is then to what extent humans can change their physical and behavioral patters during a lifetime, and not just as a matter of a global structure where humans take a central place. Going directly to plasticity, the question pertains to whether humans remain plastic all their lives, or whether they end up with stereotypic behaviors—a question that relates to the importance of education.

Is education a first start in the unfolding of a human life that nevertheless ends up in stereotypes? One cannot deny that stereotypes are a form of behavioral economy, and an important protective force, which might diminish one's plasticity. But does one need that type of protection, and if that is the case, does one need it during an entire lifetime, mixed with outbursts of plasticity?

Richard Lerner[xxxiv], child psychologist, concluded that there are many questions unanswered about the parameters of plasticity. One does, however, not know whether there are limits to a number of languages a person can speak, or the number of names of people a person may know. There seems no evidence that indicates limits in that type of plasticity. Yet, there are other questions, for instance: "is plasticity a danger for life-maintenance?" No wonder that psychological research expands its range to answer such burning questions. The need for a new look that relates psychology to genetics and neurology, to social sciences and philosophy, especially to philosophical anthropology, seems obvious.

Change is a complex issue here—a look into the structure and function of plasticity in all moments and variations of a lifetime proves it. Furthermore, changes interrelate, and that enhances the complexity of the issue even more. One process is derived from others and at the same time contributes to others who are also in a state of change. Moreover, the range of changes in the progress of time varies, although not always in an equal manner at all levels of human life.

All these insights have changed psychology since the mid-1970s. Constancy in life and continuity of expectations became a major concern when focusing on developments within a human life span. There became more dominant than ever the more or less holistic insight that processes on one level of a human psyche relate and even intertwine with processes at every other level of the organism as well as the total life situation. This newly-perceived fact reaches out to multidisciplinary research and to a new appraisal of *human nature seen on the basis of plasticity*. The interrelationships among the many levels of a human functioning show a different causality than was accepted ever before. That was especially true for a newly conceived concept of the nature of consciousness as related to brain processing and neurology.

This leads again to the already mentioned (symbolic) *interactionism*. Psychology accounted for a more important role in inner experiences than fulfilling causal control role in brain function and behavior. In other words, mental forces of a conscious mind were restored to the brain, bridging the mind-brain dualisms of the preceding years in philosophy as well as in neurology and brain research. And this also brought a different view about the 'materialistic' aspects of the relations between mind and brain. Events of the inner experience became explanatory causal constructs in their own right. The world of inner experience became recognized as a genuine domain of science.

The Whole determines fate and function of the parts, so that the *holistic* principle already exposed in preceding chapters became effective again. It implies, as Lerner shows, that the world as perceived by physical sciences is no longer solely reducible to quantum physics or any other unifying force. "Holistic properties at all different levels become causally real in their own form and have to be included in the causal account." This remark announced the end of the materialist-behaviorist era. The concept of plasticity became central to all biological and psychological studies of development. Its environment can always modify an organism.

That modifying force can pertain to modifications, which even reach into the depth of its unique genetic constellations, as recent evolutionary psychology tells us. Measuring development or behavior in response to a stimulus therefore means measuring *plasticity* (and not a single-handed response to one stimulus)—including the range of variations that can occur in an individual's development, which is a process in its own right.

Lifespan Psychology and the Sociology of the Course of Life

This reinvents, as it were, the classical studies pertaining to the *vita* of a person. Charlotte Bühler wrote as early as 1931 her first study on *Kindheit und Jugend* (Childhood and Youth), whereby plasticity was understood as an element of a phase of juvenile life. She later expanded her observations in the 1950 publication *Der Menschliche Lebenslauf* (The Course of Human Life), including the more complete life span of a human being.[xxxv] That study also engendered the typical European differentiation between life-span psychology and the sociology of a life course.

All this clearly precedes evolutionary psychology on a basis of comparison and reaching out to the duration and effects of plasticity as a major characteristic in human life. "Can humans moderate their behaviors as long as circumstances require?" was the first question of importance. The question related to issues far beyond the well-known behaviorist stimulus-response schemes. The theme "plasticity" thus escaped from the stronghold of materialism and dualism. Today, we want to know whether there is perhaps a gene for plasticity!

However, that is far-fetched and highly disputable. In the days when the question of plasticity became foundational for developmental psychology, this question was not even deemed relevant. Now, we would answer that organisms must acquire and develop plasticity in order to survive, and with the conditions of survival it becomes clear how plasticity is a developmental phenomenon, eventually influencing genetic predispositions. Are humans plastic *by definition*, as the formula 'artificial naturalness' of the philosophical anthropology suggests, or are they only *relatively* plastic?

There are undoubtedly limits to the human ability to change across a lifespan, although these limits can surprise, where stereotypical behavior could also help a human individual to survive! So plasticity could very well be a relative functional feature, and perhaps not an omnipresent, natural and universal ability, as the defenders of a philosophical anthropology wanted us to believe or to accept. It's interesting to notice how the lifespan psychology speaks about organisms in terms of "organic and inorganic levels". Organisms are "leveled" or "layered" and the behavior of an organism on a specific *level* shows different outcomes that on others.

It is meaningful to keep in mind that processes have their primary locus at one level of analysis, which relate to those having their primary locus elsewhere, that is at other levels. One is tempted to remember here the contrast between two approaches, reductionism and interactionism, whereby the first seems overtly individualistic and the second is deeply socially oriented. Richard M. Lerner suggests in view of this seemingly outmoded contrast: "We run the risk of being unclear about whether we are speaking of antecedent processes or products of these processes. Moreover, speaking repeatedly of plasticity runs the additional risk of losing sight of the fact that we are speaking only of relative plasticity, that we seek to discover both those conditions that permit and those that constrain systematic change in the structure and/or function of other variables[xxxvi]."

§ 3. Neurology, Brain Research, E-communication And E-education

Plasticity received a new context and new meanings in the days around the millennium change. This happened with the introduction of intensified brain research and the emergence of new neurological data. Research and data were possible thanks to *the development of new techniques of visualization*, because the diverse modern scanners made brain processes visual, no matter whether these processes pertained to brain activity or to brain growth.

And, what is even more important, those scanner images are not purely reproductions, or photographic images of static data. They focus on contexts and processes, and the images produced form themselves into constitutive parts of the process. In doing so, they change our standard understanding of a "copy", which was static and did not embrace any process character at all.

For instance, PET-scan images are not copies of specifically predetermined materials but elements of a process in which sender and receiver, producer and product, vision and revision are equally participating in a course of events for which we have no other name than "life". A new meaning of "image" emerged in that field of research, so that this type of visualization is nowadays the major basis for knowledge and understanding of vital processes of the human constitution. Has education profited from this progress in neurology and brain sciences? The question is justified, and the answer in the negative.

The question is the more justified because those images also produced a distinct view of *plasticity*, what could be of great importance for education. It is no exaggeration to state that these images should influence our insights in pedagogic viewpoints and in education, certainly where they are sustained by psychological research into human development. However, one has to conclude that *the mainstream of pedagogic efforts and their practical institutionalization (from Kindergarten to High School and most often to University) are based on patterns of communication that do not notice in any regard the importance of brain research, brain cell biology, or neurology.*

PET-scan Locations

Visualization techniques and the continuous flow of analyses from their results, published in monographs or journals on *nature* and *medicine,* result from a community of scientists, which embraces quite different views on human *plasticity* than educators cherish. E-educators may be an exception in this regard, because they evaluate the phenomenon of Electronically Enhanced Communication with a different perspective. And with that new enhancement of communication in general, interest in the brain as a most essential element in human life emerges. That is not a confession of materialism, nor the effect of an attitude that orders the brain far ahead of the mind or the soul!

Look at *plasticity* again. Simple images of a PET-scan make plasticity in action visible. The remarkable discovery is that there exists *no* moment in life where plasticity is *not* at work! Our impressions just depend upon the how, why, and when we visualize plasticity, not whether it concerns a substance that one can make visible now and then or with only very sophisticated machines.

This means, in other words, that plasticity is visible when we make it visible in the context we prefer or seem to be obliged to actualize. That happens in medicine, in neurology, in brain research but never in education. PET-scans seem totally alien to classrooms or teachers' consulting rooms, and it would be absurd to judge otherwise. Why? The answer goes to the constraint of codes of institutionalization: *because we ascribe a PET-scan to a hospital and not to a school; brain research and education simply do not meet or communicate on such a level!* The inherent simplification of this remark clarifies how that institutional ascription is essential and decisive, and is a barrier of importance in public life as well as in theory formation.

The PET-scan location and its institutional code is an impressive example for what the Ancient Greeks called an "episteme", and what our sociologists call an "institutionalized thought pattern". It seldom happens that one is confronted with such rigorous limiting and constraining conditions of one's own thinking! Yet it remains remarkable that notions about a human's plasticity do not play a role in our latest educative efforts. This is the more astonishing when one considers how our modern culture is fascinated by visualization in general, and pictures play a far more important role than texts—a visualized plasticity of the brain seems not to be an issue beyond brain research.

There could be a misunderstanding insofar as plasticity seems acceptable to consider in the first years of an individual's development. The hype about "the myth of the first three years" seemed significant. Early brain development was a theme in the prospect of lifelong learning, and suddenly some insight into neural connections appeared to interest progressive educators[xxxvii].

That interest faded away when it remained without the support of education institutions, and more results from brain research and neurology came to the fore. Yet, one should consider how this interest should be kept alive to the advantage of education in general and E-education in particular. Plasticity is a phenomenon not of youth, but of all phases in life. In all phases *differently*, perhaps—but that is not the decisive issue, since Heraclites taught us how the flow of life always brings new and different contexts.

So some psychological observations (quoted in preceding pages and sustained by famous psychologists such as the renowned child psychologist Richard Lerner) suggested a certain economy of psychical forces in the course of a life, which leads to stereotypes and other fixated forms of the mind. These are definitively no longer relevant. Forms of plasticity may change, but plasticity itself reaches from times before physiological birth until the physiological death of the human being. A "frozen" plasticity might be a contradiction in itself!

This observation is closely linked to the issue of *growth*. Phases and speed of growth change during a lifetime, but there is no moment where growth does not occur. Aging is growth as youth is growth—growth of the body is growth of the brain, as it is development of the mind, the cultural context of an individual, showing how the individual and the social go literally hand in hand. At this point, brain cell research and neurology come closer to each other than ever before. Neurological connections emerge during growth, whereas the death of cells also appears as a phenomenon of growth. This forms, at last, a basis for understanding the educated brain!

The Mouse at Three

The mouse is a seductive part of the computer, especially PC's, for all ages to play with. A young man of three was described as eagerly playing with the mouse and, while moving the mouse around, discovered without any problem the relation between the movements of the cursor on the screen and those of the mouse in his hand. He hardly had a firm grip on the mouse, but the movements played the major role, and they did successfully. What success?

Did the child really aim at results performed in the context of the elements of the screen, such as a game? After only a short time, this seemed the to be case. Let us emphasize: the game was not presented to him as a game, and the goals of gaming were not explained. In other words, what happened seemed quite "natural". And as we now know, the child showed with his behavior the intertwining of nature and the artifice.

One might ask many questions. Is this a very gifted child? Has it an extremely high intelligence quotient? Is it an exception in all regards—or is something else at stake here? Is it perhaps the naturalness of the mouse-design or the computer as such? Is it the family; are the parents so special and did they give that much attention to both computer and child, that the child's behavior was very special because of these special circumstances?

None of the above. The relation between child and mouse was not socially engendered, but based in the structure of a child's brain activity and the structure of the activity of mouse and computer. That is a very important observation, which provides a fascinating example for *the artificial naturalness* at work in the relation between computer and child. It leads us to the relation between the child, or better yet the brain of the child, and the computer. That causes us to have a closer look at the brain.

Brains and Computers

Is our brain a computer? The question is often asked and belongs to very different contexts. One encounters this phrase in child psychology, in developmental pedagogic, in evolutionary psychology, in child psychiatry, in cognition research, and in philosophy. Is the brain a computer, although perhaps a special one?

The three-year-old child represents a much broader question that this one. His behavior makes us reflect upon communication and education in our recent past and, above all, upon the future of our culture. Until now, we presumed that *verbal* communication fits education and other patterns of human behavior. The brain should react, respond, and reshape in such a manner that *words* are the privileged and most natural elements to communicate among humans. Our high culture has shown this in all regards—poetry, fiction, scientific prose, and rhetoric are in high esteem, often higher than sculpturing, painting, or other forms of art. How long did it take to accept photography and film as an art in comparison to painting? Words have flourished in Western culture and words are cornerstones of cultures far beyond the Western hemisphere. Other activities, such as pictures, designs, schemes, film, TV images, photo's, body movements and the like, were just accepted as illustrations accompanying the words we speak or think.

The child with the mouse shows us otherwise. The mouse is part of an electronic circuitry. There is no mouse without an effective pattern of wiring, and wiring appears to be the backbone of all E-instruments. Moreover, the wiring is the most important feature of the brain at work. The wiring of the brain and the wiring of the E-instruments (the computer in the first, but not the only, place) appear to fit. Words are more alien or at least only indirectly effective with the brain circuitry. Here is the basis for the child's behavior. The seductiveness of the mouse fits the circuitry of the brain far more directly than words ever can! Images on the computer screen are not just illustrations belonging to verbal utterances.

That is a major step in understanding E-communication and its social dimensions. Those dimensions do not relate to words—as we normally assume—but to electronically engendered issues, among which are words as well as symbols, games, or film activities. If these dimensions are interpreted as illustrations or substitutes for words, then computers remain in the corners of classrooms and the basements of family houses. *We are fed up with illustrations, but we need badly to become involved in circuitries that are out there, just like our brain!* Do not forget how our modern culture with its experience with E-communication is the first to create *resonance phenomena* that differ from verbal entities. These phenomena are a resonance to the "brain as a system of circuits", and that insight sustains the uniqueness and importance of E-communication.

This does not do away with the importance of our explanations of *words* in Chapter 3, Part III. Those fragments focused on words and, in particular, on the structures of intentionality when producing verbal utterances. Our remarks were—in the light of our above observation—*an essay to have verbal communication fit the circuitry of the active brain.* The emphasis on specific types of meaning and their implicit social structuring through words, for instance in abolishing hierarchical and even authoritarian implications, served that goal.

One should furthermore pay attention to what has been explained about the various types of verbal discourse in the context of E-devices. The distinction between "off-computer language", "pre-E-devices language" and "computer related language" is even more important where the brain circuitry is focused on. They are more than just directives within verbal communication. They should rather be understood as a medium for transition from verbal to E-communication. This shift of linguistic importance is one of the key issues in the understanding of the social implications of E-communication.

Brains as a material substance are not like computers as a material substance. That is not the meaning of the expression "brains like computers". The two demonstrate an identity of *function* and not of *substance*. Do not forget how both are elements of our own cultural history. Computers became miniaturized in the course of the last decades. That process was strongly promoted by the development of chip technology, which also induced the omnipresence of visualization techniques. There is no NASA without this visualization, offering enlarged as well as miniaturized images. There is no engineering, chemistry, biology, or archeology without such images. And, what is more closely related to brain activities, there is no illness or psychological or psychiatric disorder without a determination by means of visualization.

Computers did not only become miniaturized, but they also enlarged their format, speed, and effect. We observe the same in NASA projects or in the attempt to represent the human genome. The Human Genome Organization was based on the principle of large-scale computer generated visualization. A genome is not a simple description of a reality called "human nature", but the result of a new and revolutionary global research project.

The sequencing procedure was its heart, reading the double helix the result of this project. There is a symbolic importance here: it is the result of entrepreneurs, of big science and big business, and not of nonprofit scientific work. Appropriate sequencing cracks the coded messages in a DNA molecule, which contain the total genetic information of the species. Those messages in a DNA molecule are—as we all know—represented in strings of letters (A, C, T and G) that are abbreviations for the four nucleotides that make up the DNA.

Sequencing, visualization, and creating a nomenclature are the three essential activities in this area of research. This entire project shows how the distance to a new vision pertaining to the brain and its circuitry is not unique, but rather messages new dimensions of our knowledge about human reality.

The goals of philosophical anthropology, about which the beginning of this chapter spoke, are not lost or evaporated in the course of technical development. On the contrary: they are very much alive, but in other dimensions and in accordance with a different expressiveness.

So, one could say, in view of the meaning of words, that words are at this very moment recognized as inhabitants and stimuli of various brain circuits in which they cause different brain activities. That is totally in conformity with our exposition of the importance of words in the third chapter of this book. Words are located in the brain differently when social situations appear to be different. A PET-scan shows us the *loci* of verbal communication in brain regions. These images commit us to witness the unfolding of hitherto unknown circuits, which we traditionally perceived as social dimensions in human life.

The Range of our Capabilities

The child of three playing more or less correctly with the mouse was no exception. Many parents reported their children being able to play computer games or use the computer for all sorts of purposes long before other abilities unfolded. It seems that we have to look at the range of our mental and intellectual capabilities, which changes these days. That range is broader than ever and has a life span, from at two or three years of age to the very last years of life. Before our attempt to give a few fragments of an answer to the question of "how all this is possible", we might consider some related issues.

What about our intelligence? In other words, how do the brains of real geniuses operate? That question is not silly—remember how Einstein's brain was carefully prepared for study by coming generations! Look at the immense and immensely speculative literature on Da Vinci, Spinoza, and other so-called great minds. How did their brains function?

One aspect is that they stored information in what brain scientists call a "long-term memory". It is, however, important that they displayed the ability to organize those memories and developed a high degree of efficiency in retrieving its content. Did *they* really do that? We are not able to use a personal pronoun while describing these processes. Who did what? What identity did what? To what identity do we have to ascribe the performance of those brain activities[xxxviii]? The question's answer only points at the limits of our grammar and, with that grammar, of our understanding! In any case, one can conclude that geniuses bring long-term memory into short-term use! Do geniuses do that? Did the three-year-old child playing with the computer mouse do that?

What about genetics? In other words, do special genetic predispositions bring some of us to master this transition of long-term memory into short-term use? If genetics determine humans entirely, then we all are mediocre and hardly differentiated beings! One can only conclude that individual efforts enhance structural changes of the brain, and that these go with changes of brain functions. Yes, our brains change when we are at work, and those changes might improve that work! But part of this process is the result of some sort of inherited determination, whereas other parts (which we can not exactly indicate or master) result from exercises, learning, and development. Nature goes with nurture, genes with environment.

More details remain concealed. What brain researchers and developmental psychologists conclude from the actions of geniuses, great musicians, painters, or scientists is that they achieve higher levels of control over every aspect of their performance in a chosen field. This achievement seems to be highly stimulated by internal motivation, and that motivation is often the result of education making rigid training inhabit the person involved. In order to cope with this strong motivation, researchers conclude, these persons encode, store, manage, and manipulate information quickly and efficiently. Their brain activities thus correlate with a strong and stable intentionality.

Learning and education belong to the factors involved in those brain processes. There is no way to escape this conclusion. The seduction of the task to fulfill (for instance playing with the mouse) goes with the preparedness to concentrate on *this* and not on something else. One notes that, between three and five years of age, brain changes to prepare for that attitude can occur under the condition that an environmentally supported willingness appears and is fortified! Educators should notice this, and E-education profits from this *early plasticity* when they create E-environments for the purpose of brain change and willful plasticity effects.

This is no longer the result of speculations or of extrapolations of our knowledge pertaining to a functioning brain. All this became visible: functional MRI's show nowadays how the brain has "individual signatures". It implies that brain activities vary from person to person, and from one task to another task performed by the same brain. Those "signatures" can set the stage for individualized E-education programs, which make E-education even more effective. Here we are very near to the conclusion we ventured to formulate before: *scans can indeed be admitted in E-education centers, and help determine the "state of brain" as a starting point for an E-education program.*

The Brain and the Skull: Inside and Outside

With this new vision there also changes the importance of words, human relations, and educational settings, that is, the social dimensions of E-communication. Look for a moment at the brain itself. The brain inhabited the human skull until only a few decades ago. The brain was well kept there, and represented most powerfully *a world inside*. The brain was, not unlike the heart, a reality and a metaphor for this sacred inside—an untouchable area of human essence and human dignity. The two symbolized a limit, which could neither be touched nor transgressed. Metaphysical dimensions are at stake in this context.

Well, today the skull does not need to be opened in order to obtain knowledge of the functioning brain. If the brain is opened, it is seldom for observing how its organs function! A surgically opened brain does enable us seldom to see *what is going on* in terms of neurology. New imaging techniques became a source of knowledge, they opened the brain with different means, non-physiologically and unveiled issues, which are altogether elements of a living and functioning brain.

The dead brain of Einstein is of no value for brain research anymore. His well-kept brain is just a symbol of an outmoded science and a dead language. As a consequence, the mind/brain discussion in philosophy is a past station on the way to newly acquired knowledge about the brain as a centre of human life. Hamlet's hand, holding the skull, is still full of poetic actuality, but his looks are different, his words or thoughts are hardly recognizable and his metaphysics no longer an agenda for the good life.

So there are very different definitions of cognition in modern science. These are still in the frame of stimulus-response schemes, but no longer represent a philosophical viewpoint called materialism. They generally pertain to the ability of a brain and its neuronal system to attend, identify, and act on complex stimuli. What else does the brain, the human body, the human existence, when it is reading these lines? Or, to formulate an even more recent question: does the ongoing multitasking of children at school, scientists in their labs, or coach potatoes watching TV do anything else? They are all living in various forms of cognition, perhaps the most widespread environment of the modern mind. Complex stimuli deliver cognition—but their outcome may be very different in sort and quality.

There is, however, one more issue to mention. The remarks of this section did not at any time mention differences between good and bad, normal and abnormal, intelligent and non-intelligent or other categories that are standard in the language of social communication. There is no longer a prevailing emphasis on the abnormal, on disease and dysfunction as a means to acquire knowledge of the normal. We no longer need sick brains to know about illness, no longer blossoming psychiatric phenomena to understand a deviant life. The average individual is enough.

Developmental neurosciences have shown how brains are in a continuous state of change, and that those changes can be changed under the influence of an environment or (what is principally the same) through the influence of other persons: psychiatrists, educators, or social workers. These views on the human brain make us concentrate on the average like we concentrated in earlier days on the 'healthy' or the 'sick'. ADHD, to mention an example, appears to be a variation of the average, and our therapy will be a catastrophe if we one-sidedly treat the ADHD person with without recognizing this! A new environment (preferably an E-environment where words have other meanings and are framed in related circuits) will meet the needs of the person, which are no longer qualified as 'special'!

Plasticity Again

So we are back to plasticity! Brain mechanisms are constantly involved in translation. Sensory and other capacities result from those translations and transferences. Information that stems from the environment is transferred from one sensory channel to another, and that ability of transference can be stimulated by influences from "outside". The word "outside" stems, however, from a period in which the brain inhabited the skull. In that location, it could not participate in the life of knowledge.

Today, we have other access to and other information about the brain, for instance not resulting from patients with a brain contusion, or specific diseases, but from scans. Those reveal how touch sensations can become transferred to areas of visual perception, so that the person impaired in feeling can "see feelings" (a variation on what Oliver Sacks could have said). The same sense-fields can become activated through a special environment in E-education centers, which is designed to enhance reading or math capacities. Another example of this unique transference of sensory channels to others is in learning to know one's own body. That should be taught beyond the classical schemes of biology that schools demonstrate with charts, words, and films.

The brain's ability to transfer from channel to channel and field to field is a basis for honoring and evaluating human plasticity. It is not surprising that the brain's capacity for change exists life-long—not merely from three to twenty years of age. This has enormous consequences for the social dimensions of E-communication. The E-guided environmental influences on a person are effective in all phases of a course of life. Exposure to a technically enhanced environment beyond words and maps corresponds with technologically driven changes in the brain. That is a most promising and valuable basis for E-education reaching out to impaired persons of all ages, and to cope with the phenomena that belong to specific illnesses. Those promises belong to the in-depth meaning of the word "social" when we speak about the social dimensions of E-education. "Social" means principally "artificial naturalness" and it is the artifice that brings change!

§ 4. The Connected Citizen.

The two are identical as far as their meaning is concerned: citizens as goals of education are persons living in an "artificial naturalness" and their "connectedness" is a basic ingredient of precisely this type of naturalness. A major consequence is that *one cannot conceive of any modern citizenship without E-communicative skills and practices*. The first chapter underlined four different influences on new citizenship experiences. We recapitulate those four.

a) First, there is a citizenship that relates to new features of *institutions*. They are visible in the recent practices of *bureaucracy* and *administration,* where both became unthinkable without E-communication.

Citizens now face 'geographically non-identifiable institutions through the Internet, a situation that, especially for senior citizens, is an alarming experience. Institutions incorporate new techniques, many of them based on electronics, and have a different ritual to access via electronically designed programs.

Traditional clients of such institutions are really afraid to just become electronically served, where they normally experience a moment of valuable social contacts. The evolution of electronic banking was introduced as an example, in which banks receive clients whereas in earlier days a personal relationship was made possible. That evolution goes to 'connected citizens' as a major ingredient of social life.

b) New features of citizenship relate furthermore to *genetics*, often combined with new insights of neurosciences and sustained by electronic techniques of visualization. These were the objects of our above considerations. There is more than one issue of change. Consider again how genetics produce a new way of *thinking about social relations.* Problems of determinism come up, and the individual carries the weight to no longer not belong to any individualistic category, although the expression "genetic constellation" suggests the contrary. But even that constellation is the product of computer techniques.

Genetics changed the fundamental concept of *freedom*. How can one feel free with an unknown and unexplored package of electronically engendered information that relates at least partially to illness, heritage, family responsibility, and death? Do citizens ever possess enough knowledge to practice their freedom?

Genetics shed a new light on each individual's *genealogical tree*. It becomes difficult to perceive oneself in the light of genetics as an *identity with others* in a genealogical tree! It is I who stand on the shoulders of my family, sometimes with one foot, sometimes with both feet!

And genetics change *patterns of social relationships*. This is most manifest in the genetic consult and counseling, but it also starts to play a role in education. Medical counseling pertains to *statistical* data and *probabilities* created by electronically performed analyses. Education might in our foreseeable future need brain scans to decide on the appropriate education approach. Everything depends in that case on the *interpretation* of statistics and images. However, all in all one must conclude that citizens' connectedness is the major condition for the described effects of genetics.

c) Modern citizenship needs an increased awareness of the (natural and artificially constructed) *environment*. Citizens are stimulated to engage in new dimensions of responsibility for their environment, but also have to cope with the artificial character of their environment. Citizens create an elaborate understanding about the fact that their relation to the environment is not a subject-object relationship. Their environment is, in other words, not a *thing* to dispose of freely. Citizens are only citizens because they can *inhabit* the environment; they are together with that environment, and should take care as if it concerns a partner. On that level of understanding, they are challenged to practice the intertwining of the artificial and the natural. No need to explicitly underline how this practice is conditioned by the ability of citizens to be connected, and to live a connected life, develop a respective life style and an appropriated self-understanding.

d) A *fourth* type of citizenship relates to *learning*. Stimuli to propagate "active citizenship" aim at participation in a "learning society". The latter involves (1) a type of *learning* that differs fundamentally from *teaching* or *instructing*, a type that is (2) circular, so that electronic devices and social institutions learn from the learning processes they instigate, and (3) long lasting, often defined as "life-long". Social positions change accordingly (workplace home-work, e-technological divide), and age barriers tend to be abolished in the learning situation (the elder have to learn as well as the young). We neglected "adult learning" as a specific social form and conceived it only as a form of learning "at a later age". *Learning society* is the concept that replaces the concept of a *contractual society* because the latter represents the concept of exchange of fixed positions! How could learning develop beyond connectedness, one should ask.

These reflections upon new forms of citizenship include a turn away from *individualism* towards new practices of communication. The turn itself is an important contribution for making electronic communication possible, and a fruitful conceptualization in view of foreseeable technological developments, which reach from a new understanding of the circuitry of the brain to the many ways our social dimensions of communication fit these new concepts. The "fit" is the greatest challenge in view of all social dimensions involved in E-communication.

Endnotes Chapter One

[i] Sherry Turkle: **The Second Self: Computers and the Human Spirit**, New York 1984.

[ii] As in the works of Gurwitsch, Mead, Parsons, Goffmann, Berger & Luckmann who were treating this symbolic interactionism as a new perspective on the multiple meanings of a self, the nature of the human self, and communication in role-reversing, the creation of new meanings, or immersions in music, literature and the arts—whereby electronic devices were fundamentally neglected.

[iii] Sir Leon Bagrit: **The Age of Automation: The BBC Reith Lectures** 1964, New York 1965.

[iv] Seymour Papert: **The Children's Machine: Rethinking School in the Age of the Computer**, New York 1993. Chapter 1, see also his: **Mindstorms: Children, Computers, and Powerful Ideas**, NY 1993 (first edition 1980).

[v] Bagrit, **Lectures** (see note iii), pages 36–48.

[vi] B.F.Skinner: *The Phylogeny and Ontology of Behavior*, in **Science**, 1966, *153*, p 1205 ff.

[vii] B. F. Skinner, **The Technology of Teaching.** New York 1968, p. 3–5.

[viii] M. McLuhan: **Understanding Media: The Extensions of Man.** London 1969 [1964], p.371.

ix Skinner, **Technology** (see note vii), p. 21.

x Seymour Papert: **The Children's Machine.**, New York 1993, p.4 ff. What is said here about video games is also valid for electronic pocket calculators. Both lead children to computers in an almost natural way.

xi S. Papert: **The Children's Machine** (see note xi), page 114.

xii W. James: Talks to Teachers on Psychology, New York 1899.

xiii Papert: **The Children's Machine** (see note xi), p. 5 ff.

xiv Tim Morrison: **The Magic of Interactive Entertainment**, Indianapolis, SAMS Publishing, 1994.

xv Charles Taylor: *Atomism* in: **Communitarianism and Individualism**, (Shl. Avineri & A.De-Shalit, Eds) Oxford U.P. 1992, p. 43 ff.

xvi See for example the full page advertisement of the Bluewater Network in the NYTimes, December 22, 2004, about the exorbitant gas consumption of cars build by Ford Motor Company.

Endnotes Chapter Two

xvii A. Cohen: **The Natural and the Supernatural Jew**", Pantheon Books, New York 1962

xviii Ludwig Feuerbach: **Principles of a Philosophy of the Future**, 1843.

xix F. Rosenzweig: **Briefe.** Schocken Verlag, Berlin 1935. Brief 360, p. 448.

xx Nahum N. Glatzer: **Franz Rosenzweig: His Life and Thought,** New York 1961; Notice, that the history of the Lehrhaus (1919–1926) and in particular of its ideological backgrounds, has not yet been researched and interpreted. Important is in this context the contribution of Buber to the Lehrhaus, and also of interest the relations of Rosenzweig and Buber to the Frankfurt University. Rosenzeig's 1922 chair for Jewish Religion and Ethics was only 1924 fulfilled by Buber, since Rosenzweig's terminal illness left his for 1922 announced teachings vacant. Cf. Rita van de Sandt: **Martin Bubers Bildnerische Tätigkeit zwischen den beiden Weltkriegen,** Stuttgart 1977, p. 80 ff.

xxi F. Rosenzweig: *Bildung und kein Ende,* **Kleinere Schriften,** Schocken Verlag, Berlin 1937, p. 90, in Glatzer (quoted in note xx.) p. 226.

xxii G. Scholem: **Major Trends in Jewish Mysticism,** New York 1941.

xxiii J. Fleischmann, in: Le problème de Martin Buber, in **Revue Philosophique de la France et de L' Étranger,** 1959, Nr 84, p. 351 emphasizes that Bubers philosophical attitude showed clearer in Religious Studies than in sociology or psychology.

xxiv F. Rosenzweig: *Bildung und kein Ende,* **Kleinere Schriften,** Schocken Verlag, Berlin 1937, p. 90.

xxv This overshadows the Western desire to *possess* knowledge about being and reality before utterances can be performed. That desire, absent in Hebraic traditions, suppresses how the other presents reality as it is.

xxvi M. Buber: **Briefwechsel aus sieben Jahrzehnten, Bd. II: 1918–1938,** Grete Schaeder [Ed.] Heidelberg 1973, Brief 103, not dated, possibly just before 09.14.1922.

Endnotes Chapter Three

xxvii L.Wittgenstein: **Philosophical Investigations,** Oxford 1953, § 89, and §§109,129.

xxviii J.C.Smuts: **Holism and Evolution,** New York 1926.

xxix One finds an elaborate representation of the philosophical problems involved in questions pertaining to the *Holon* in philosophy, law and medicine, in: Jan M. Broekman: *Holism, Law, and the Principle of Expressibility* in: **Rechtstheorie,** Vol 21, 1990, pages 415–440. Issues of communication and education parallel those insights.

xxx J. Habermas: **The Theory of Communicative Action,** (2 Vols), Beacon Press 1984–87

xxxi John Searle: **Speech Acts,** Cambridge (UK) 1970, pages 20 f.

Endnotes Chapter Five

xxxii This chapter follows in a surprisingly harmonious mode the preceding pages, written as a 1995 PhD thesis; they show the reader how the present is better equipped to enhance the meaning and scope of the earlier texts.

xxxiii H. Plessner: **Die Stufen des Organischen und der Mensch,** Berlin 1928.

xxxiv Richard M. Lerner: **On the nature of human plasticity,** Cambridge UP, 1984, p. 168 f.

xxxv Charlotte Bühler: **Kindheit und Jugend,** Leipzig 1931. See also Bühler: **Der menschliche Lebenslauf,** Göttingen 1950. Modern lifespan psychology embraces four principles:
i) growth, stability, and change in behavior occur throughout life; (ii) there is a continuous interplay between growth (gains) and decline (losses) in ontogeny; (iii) selection, optimization, and compensation constitute fundamental elements of development; and (iv) there are age-associated changes in adaptive potential (plasticity). All psychological development is embedded in a biological, historical, and cultural context. The overarching architecture of human ontogeny reflects the dialectical interplay of these components and their evolution.

xxxvi One should think of Nicolai Hartmann's unique way, different from Max Scheler and other philosophers of his time, to develop a philosophical theory about all that *is*, an *ontology*,as "Schichtenlehre", a theory of layers, or levels. H.Spiegelberg comments in his famous publication: **The Phenomenological Movement,** 1963, p.309 ff: ""it will be best to look first at the type of topics and problems which Hartmann took up under the time-honored name. They comprise not only being qua being, i.e., the most general concept of what is (*das Seiende*), but existence (*Dasein*) and essence (*Sosein*), which he calls *Seinsmomente,* and the types of being designated by the adjectives 'real' and 'ideal,' named *Seinsweisen,* all of which are discussed in the first volume of the ontological tetralogy. The second volume deals with the modes of being (*Seinsmodi*) such as possibility and actuality, necessity and contingency, impossibility and unreality—particularly impressive and perhaps the most original part of the set. The next major theme is the categories, first the general ones applying to all the strata (*Schichten*) of the real world and explored in the third volume (*Der Aufbau der realen Welt*), then the special categories pertaining only to limited areas, such as nature, which Hartmann takes op in the final work. Finally, there are the categories peculiar to the realm of cultural entities (*geistiges Sein*) which he discussed in a work whose publication actually preceded the ontological tetralogy."

xxxvi Richard M. Lerner: **On the Nature of Human Plasticity** (see note iii) p.6 ff. and Mary Jane West-Eberhard: **Developmental Plasticity and Evolution.** Oxford UP 2003, as well as Catherine Malabou & Lisabeth During: **The Future of Hegel: Plasticity, Temporality and Dialectic,** Routledge, London 2004.

xxxvii John T. Bruer: **The Myth of the First Three Years**, New York 1999, p. 65 f.

xxxviii This observation is important in the light of complaints about school-children's attention span, which is characterized by a short-term impulse and horizon, lack of confidence, and self-reliance. Should teachers, e-teachers in particular, not focus memory-organization and the efficiency of retrieving the memorized materials the same way it can happen in their brains?

LITERATURE

Bagrit, Sir Leon: **The Age of Automation: The BBC Reith Lectures 1964**, New York 1965.

Broekman, Jan M.: *Holism, Law, and the Principle of Expressibility* in: **Rechtstheorie,** Vol 21, 1990.

Jan M. Broekman: **The Virtual in E-education,** New York 2004.

Buber, Martin: Briefwechsel aus sieben Jahrzehnten, Bd. II: 1918–1938, Grete Schaeder [Ed.] Heidelberg 1973.

Cohen, Abraham: **The Natural and the Supernatural Jew,** New York 1964.

Feuerbach, Ludwig: **Principles of a Philosophy of the Future,** 1843.

Fleischmann, Johan in: *Le problème de Martin Buber*, in **Revue Philosophique de la France et de L' Étranger,** 1959.

Foox, Michael H.: **Devices in E-education,** New York 2004.

Glatzer, Nahum N.: **Franz Rosenzweig: His Life and Thought,** New York 1961.

Habermas Jürgen: **The Theory of Communicative Action**, (2 Vols), Beacon Press 1984–87.

James, William: **Talks to Teachers on Psychology,** New York 1899.

Lilla, Mark: *A Battle for Religion* in **New York Review of Books,** Dec. 2002, Vol XLIX.

Lilla, Mark: *Leo Strauss: The European*, in **New York Review of Books,** Oct. 2004, Vol.LI

McLuhan, Marshall: **Understanding Media: The Extensions of Man.** London 1969 [1964(1)].

Morrison, Tim: **The Magic of Interactive Entertainment**, Indianapolis, SAMS Publishing, 1994.

Papert, Seymour: **Mindstorms: Children, Computers, and Powerful Ideas,** NY 1993 [1980 (1)]

Papert, Seymour: **The Children's Machine: Rethinking School in the Age of the Computer**, New York 1993.

Rosenzweig, Franz: *Bildung und kein Ende,* **Kleinere Schriften**, Schocken Verlag, Berlin 1937.

Rosenzweig, Franz: **Briefe.** Schocken Verlag, Berlin 1935.

Sandt, Rita van de: **Martin Bubers Bildnerische Tätigkeit zwischen den beiden Weltkriegen,** Stuttgart 1977.

Scholem, Gershom: **Major Trends in Jewish Mysticism,** New York 1941.

Searle, John: **Speech Acts,** Cambridge (UK) 1997.

Skinner, B.F., **The Technology of Teaching.** New York 1968.

Skinner, B.F.: *The Phylogeny and Ontology of Behavior*, in **Science**, 1966, *153.*

Smuts, Jan C.: **Holism and Evolution**, New York 1926.

Strauss, Leo: **Spinoza's Critique of Religion**, Schocken Books, New York 1982.

Taylor, Charles: *Atomism* in: **Communitarianism and Individualism**, (S. Avineri & A.De-Shalit, Eds) Oxford U.P. 1992.

Taylor, Charles: **Modern Social Imageries,** Duke UP, Durham & London 2004.

Turkle, Sherry: **The Second Self: Computers and the Human Spirit**, New York 1984.

Wittgenstein, Ludwig: **Philosophical Investigations**, Oxford 1953.

To order additional copies of this book, contact:

IIS LLC AT;
 WWW.MIIL.ORG
 MF@MIIL.ORG

OR:

 IUNIVERSE™
 WWW.IUNIVERSE.COM

978-0-595-35656-0
0-595-35656-7